Guide to Food Storage

Follow this guide for food storage, and you can be sure that what's in your freezer, refrigerator, and pantry is fresh-tasting and ready to use in recipes.

In the Freezer (at -10° to 0° F)

DAIRY

Cheese, hard	6 months
Cheese, soft	6 months
Egg substitute, unopened	1 year
Egg whites	1 year
Egg yolks	1 year
Ice cream, sherbet	1 month

FRUITS AND VEGETABLES

Commercially frozen fruits	1 year
Commercially frozen vegetables	8 to 12 months

MEATS, POULTRY, AND SEAFOOD

Beef, Lamb, Pork, and Veal

Chops, uncooked	4 to 6 months
Ground and stew meat, uncooked	3 to 4 months
Ham, fully cooked, half	1 to 2 months
Roasts, uncooked	4 to 12 months
Steaks, uncooked	6 to 12 months

Poultry

All cuts, cooked	4 months
Boneless or bone-in pieces, uncooked	9 months

Seafood

Fish, fatty, uncooked	2 to 3 months
Fish, lean, uncooked	6 months

In the Refrigerator (at 34° to 40° F)

DAIRY

Butter	1 to 3 months
Buttermilk	1 to 2 weeks
Cheese, hard, wedge, opened	6 months
Cheese, semihard, block, opened	3 to 4 weeks
Cream cheese, fat-free, light, and $1/3$-less-fat	2 weeks
Egg substitute, opened	3 days
Fresh eggs in shell	3 to 5 weeks

MEATS, POULTRY, AND SEAFOOD

Beef, Lamb, Pork, and Veal

Ground and stew meat, uncooked	1 to 2 days
Roasts, uncooked	3 to 5 days
Steaks and chops, uncooked	3 to 5 days

Chicken, Turkey, and Seafood

All cuts, uncooked	1 to 2 days

FRUITS AND VEGETABLES

Apples, beets, cabbage, carrots, celery, citrus fruits, eggplant, and parsnips	2 to 3 weeks
Apricots, asparagus, berries, cauliflower, cucumbers, mushrooms, okra, peaches, pears, peas, peppers, plums, salad greens, and summer squash	2 to 4 days
Corn, husked	1 day

In the Pantry (keep these at room temperature for 6 to 12 months)

BAKING AND COOKING STAPLES

Baking powder

Biscuit and baking mixes

Broth, canned

Cooking spray

Honey

Mayonnaise, fat-free, low-fat, and light (unopened)

Milk, canned evaporated fat-free

Milk, nonfat dry powder

Mustard, prepared (unopened)

Oils, olive and vegetable

Pasta, dried

Peanut butter

Rice, instant and regular

Salad dressings, bottled (unopened)

Seasoning sauces, bottled

Tuna, canned

FRUITS, LEGUMES, AND VEGETABLES

Fruits, canned

Legumes (beans, lentils, peas), dried or canned

Tomato products, canned

Vegetables, canned

weightwatchers®

easy everyday favorites

Oxmoor House®

ISBN 13: 978-0-8487-3980-5
ISBN 10: 0-8487-3980-9
Library of Congress Control Number: 2012953460
Printed in the United States of America
First printing 2013

Be sure to check with your health-care provider before making any changes in your diet.

WEIGHT WATCHERS for services and **PointsPlus®** are the registered trademarks of Weight Watchers International, Inc., and are used with permission by Time Home Entertainment Inc.

Oxmoor House

Editorial Director: Leah McLaughlin
Creative Director: Felicity Keane
Brand Manager: Katie McHugh
Senior Editor: Heather Averett
Managing Editor: Rebecca Benton

Weight Watchers® Easy Everyday Favorites

Editor: Shaun Chavis
Art Director: Claire Cormany
Senior Designer: J. Shay McNamee
Director, Test Kitchen: Elizabeth Tyler Austin
Assistant Directors, Test Kitchen: Julie Christopher, Julie Gunter
Recipe Developers and Testers: Wendy Ball, RD, Victoria E. Cox, Tamara Goldis, Stefanie Maloney, Callie Nash, Karen Rankin, Leah Van Deren
Recipe Editor: Alyson Moreland Haynes
Food Stylists: Margaret Monroe Dickey, Catherine Crowell Steele
Photography Director: Jim Bathie
Senior Photographer: Helene Dujardin
Senior Photo Stylist: Kay E. Clarke
Photo Stylist: Mindi Shapiro Levine
Assistant Photo Stylist: Mary Louise Menendez
Production Manager: Tamara Nall Wilder
Senior Production Manager: Greg A. Amason

Contributors

Editor: Carolyn Land Williams, PhD, RD
Designer: Cathy Robbins
Project Editor: Lacie Pinyan
Copy Editors: Dolores Hydock, Erica Midkiff
Proofreaders: Lauren Brooks, Carmine Loper
Indexer: Mary Ann Laurens
Recipe Developers and Testers: Erica Hopper, Tonya Johnson, Kyra Moncrief, Kathleen Royal Phillips
Photographer: Daniel Taylor
Photo Stylist: Leslie Simpson
Food Stylist: Ana Price Kelly
Interns: Megan Branagh, Frances Gunnells, Susan Kemp, Sara Lyon, Staley McIlwain, Jeffrey Preis, Emily Robinson, Maria Sanders, Julia Sayers

Time Home Entertainment Inc.

Publisher: Jim Childs
VP, Strategy & Business Development: Steven Sandonato
Executive Director, Marketing Services: Carol Pittard
Executive Director, Retail & Special Sales: Tom Mifsud
Director, Bookazine Development & Marketing: Laura Adam
Executive Publishing Director: Joy Butts
Associate Publishing Director: Megan Pearlman
Finance Director: Glenn Buonocore
Associate General Counsel: Helen Wan

Cover: Quick Steak Fajitas (page 109)

Contents

Everyday Favorites for Every Occasion

Everyone has a few go-to recipes—those no-fail favorites that are easy to prepare and that everyone loves. The problem with many of these dishes, though, is they can often be high in calories and fat, leaving a lot to be desired nutritionally if you're trying to lose weight. *Weight Watchers® Easy, Everyday Favorites* offers more than 180 delicious recipes that are sure to become your new favorites. Not only are these dishes tasty, but they're also a snap to prepare—and they easily fit into the *Weight Watchers* plan. In fact, 140 of the recipes have a ***PointsPlus®*** value of 6 or less.

Easy, Everyday Favorites is organized into quick-reference chapters, so whether you need a family-friendly entrée or a side dish for a backyard cookout, you've got it all right at your fingertips. For each recipe, you'll also find a complete nutritional analysis with ***PointsPlus*** values, prep and cook times, a menu or grocery list, and a game plan to help you strategize and keep meal preparation simple.

Here's how a few of our favorite recipes can fit into any day: Jump-start your day with Banana–Macadamia Nut Pancakes (***PointsPlus*** value of 4, page 28) or a classic like Eggs Benedict (***PointsPlus*** value of 5, page 50). Or take a Berry-Banana Smoothie (***PointsPlus*** value of 4, page 59) with you on the go for breakfast or a snack.

When lunchtime calls, don't get stuck in the takeout trap. Instead, sink your teeth into an Apple and Cheddar Grilled Cheese (***PointsPlus*** value of 8, page 74) or Tropical Shrimp Salad (***PointsPlus*** value of 7, page 91). Then, please the whole family with Quick Steak Fajitas (***PointsPlus*** value of 7, page 109) or Creamy Macaroni and Cheese (***PointsPlus*** value of 7, page 97).

For special occasions, treat your sweet tooth while staying on plan with Turtle Brownies (***PointsPlus*** value of 4, page 175) or Key Lime Pie Ice Cream (***PointsPlus*** value of 6, page 181).

With all these ideas, you can throw together tasty meals and snacks every day. So get ready to enjoy a whole new set of home-cooked favorites that are both simple to prepare and low in ***PointsPlus*** values.

Want to Learn More about *Weight Watchers*?

Weight Watchers is the world's leading provider of weight management services that has been helping people successfully lose weight for 50 years. At *Weight Watchers*, weight management is a partnership that combines our knowledge with your efforts. For more information about the *Weight Watchers* program and a meeting nearest you, call **1-800-651-6000** or visit online at **www.weightwatchers.com**

Five Secrets for Delicious, Easy Meals Every Day

Each recipe includes step-by-step instructions that walk you through preparation, but here are a few things you can do prior to cooking to make putting meals on the table even easier.

1. Plan for the week, and use menus.

Look at your week's activities, and decide which days you're able to cook. Then plan the dishes you'll prepare, and create a grocery list for the week. This will take a little time initially, but it will pay off later in the week and will become easier each time.

2. Work the game plan.

Make sure to read the game plan provided with each appetizer and entrée recipe. Many recipes have some downtime during which you can prepare a side dish; the game plan will point this out so you can use your time in the kitchen efficiently.

3. Keep everyday staples in your kitchen.

Having basic ingredients on hand makes meal preparation even simpler. Below is a list of basics we recommend; once your pantry is stocked, you'll mainly shop for produce, meat and seafood, and dairy items each week. Make a note when any of the staples are running low or about to expire.

- *Broth: fat-free, lower-sodium beef, chicken, and vegetable*
- *Cooking spray: regular and olive oil–flavored*
- *Oil: olive, canola, and sesame*
- *Canned olives*
- *Bottled capers*
- *Mayonnaise: light and fat-free*
- *Mustard: Dijon and stone-ground*
- *Salad dressings: light, reduced-fat, and fat-free*

- *Baking powder*
- *Baking soda*
- *Cornstarch*
- *Flour: all-purpose, bread, self-rising, and whole-wheat*
- *Sugar: granulated and brown*
- *Salt and pepper*
- *Kosher salt*
- *Dried herbs and spices*
- *Garlic*

- *Canned tomato products*
- *Lower-sodium soy sauce*
- *Vinegar: balsamic, cider, red wine, rice wine, and white wine*
- *Vanilla extract*
- *Butter*
- *Eggs*
- *Fat-free milk*
- *Lemons*

4. Bookmark top recipes.

Mark your favorite recipes so you can quickly refer to them. Make a note of any garnishes you use and what you serve with the dish. Soon, you'll have a personalized collection of delicious go-to recipes.

5. Make healthy side dishes easy.

Round out the menu with quick sides that need little cooking or prep. All items on the list below have low **PointsPlus** values, so many are also great snack choices.

Fruits
- *Fresh fruit, whole or cut up*
- *Canned fruit in juice*
- *Unsweetened applesauce*

Dairy Items
- *Fat-free milk*
- *Reduced-fat cheese sticks or wedges*
- *Fat-free yogurt*

Vegetables
- *Baby carrots*
- *Cucumber slices*
- *Celery sticks*
- *Washed and cut vegetables in steamable bags*
- *Frozen vegetables in steamable bags*
- *Bagged salad greens*

Grains
- *Whole-wheat, reduced-fat crackers*
- *Whole-wheat English muffins*
- *Whole-wheat pasta (couscous, rotini, spaghetti)*
- *Wild and brown rice*

About the Recipes

Weight Watchers® *Easy, Everyday Favorites* gives you the nutrition facts you need to stay on track. Every recipe in this book has been evaluated by our Test Kitchen staff and received our highest endorsement. Each recipe also includes a *PointsPlus*® value. For more information on Weight Watchers, see page 4.

Each recipe has a list of nutrients— including calories, fat, saturated fat, protein, carbohydrates, dietary fiber, cholesterol, iron, sodium, and calcium— as well as a serving size and the number of servings. This information makes it easy for you to use the recipes for any weight-loss program that you choose to follow. Measurements are abbreviated g (grams) and mg (milligrams). Nutritional values used in our calculations come from either The Food Processor, Version 8.9 (ESHA Research), or are provided by food manufacturers.

Numbers are based on these assumptions:
• Unless otherwise indicated, meat, poultry, and fish always refer to skinned, boned, and cooked servings.
• When we give a range for an ingredient (3 to 3½ cups flour, for instance), we calculate using the lesser amount.
• Some alcohol calories evaporate during heating; the analysis reflects this.
• Only the amount of marinade absorbed by the food is used in calculations.
• Garnishes and optional ingredients are not included in an analysis.

Safety Note: Cooking spray should never be used near direct heat. Always remove a pan from heat before spraying it with cooking spray.

A Note on Diabetic Exchanges: You may notice that the nutrient analysis for each recipe does not include Diabetic Exchanges. Most dietitians and diabetes educators are now teaching people with diabetes to count total carbohydrates at each meal and snack, rather than counting exchanges. Counting carbohydrates gives people with diabetes more flexibility in their food choices and seems to be an effective way to manage blood glucose.

PointsPlus values

PointsPlus uses the latest scientific research to create a program that goes far beyond traditional calorie counting to give people the edge they need to lose weight and keep it off in a fundamentally healthier way. The program is designed to educate and encourage people to make choices that focus on foods that create a sense of satisfaction and are more healthful. *PointsPlus* values are calculated for foods based on their protein, fiber, fat, and carbohydrate content. This *PointsPlus* formula takes into account how these nutrients are processed by the body and helps you select foods that are both nutritious and satisfying! For more about the *PointsPlus* Program, visit www.weightwatchers.com

Appetizers & Beverages

Menu
PointsPlus value
per serving: 3

**Grilled Corn
and Black Bean Salsa**

1 ounce baked tortilla chips
PointsPlus value
per serving: 3

Game Plan

1. While corn cooks:
  • Rinse and drain beans.
  • Combine other salsa
    ingredients.

2. Cut corn off cob, and add
    to salsa.

Grilled Corn and Black Bean Salsa

prep: 2 minutes • **cook:** 12 minutes   *PointsPlus* value per serving: 0

Placing the corn directly on the grill rack allows the kernels to develop a slightly charred golden color on the outside and a smoky grilled flavor on the inside. Increase the serving size to 1 cup and the salsa becomes a side dish with a *PointsPlus* value of 2. Serve the salsa alongside grilled fish, meat, or chicken.

 2   medium ears shucked corn
Cooking spray
 ½   teaspoon salt
 ¼   teaspoon pepper
 2   tablespoons red wine vinegar
 1   teaspoon olive oil
 ½   teaspoon ground cumin
 1   (15-ounce) can black beans, rinsed and drained
 1   large tomato, chopped

1. Preheat grill to medium-high heat.
2. Coat 2 ears corn with cooking spray; sprinkle with salt and pepper. Place corn on grill rack; cover and grill 6 minutes on each side or until slightly charred.
3. While corn cooks, combine vinegar and next 4 ingredients in a medium bowl. Cut corn off cob, and add to bowl; toss well. **Yield:** 20 servings (serving size: ¼ cup).

Per serving: CALORIES 19; FAT 0.4g (sat 0.1g, mono 0.2g, poly 0.1g); PROTEIN 0.9g; CARB 3.7g; FIBER 1g; CHOL 0mg; IRON 0.3mg; SODIUM 83mg; CALC 6mg

Fresh Crab Dip

prep: 15 minutes

PointsPlus value per serving: 1

Serve this dip with cracked pepper–flavored water crackers or toasted baguette slices.

 4 ounces tub-style light cream cheese, softened (about ½ cup)
⅓ cup fat-free sour cream
 1 tablespoon prepared horseradish, divided
¼ teaspoon salt
¼ cup chili sauce
¾ teaspoon fresh lemon juice
¼ teaspoon Worcestershire sauce
 4 ounces lump crabmeat, shell pieces removed
 2 tablespoons finely chopped green onions

1. Combine cream cheese, sour cream, 1½ teaspoons horseradish, and salt in a medium bowl; stir until smooth. Spread mixture in a shallow bowl.
2. Combine 1½ teaspoons horseradish, chili sauce, lemon juice, and Worcestershire sauce in a small bowl, stirring well. Spoon a thin layer over cream cheese mixture. Mound crabmeat in center, and sprinkle with green onions. **Yield:** 12 servings (serving size: about 2 tablespoons).

Per serving: CALORIES 46; FAT 1.8g (sat 1.2g, mono 0.2g, poly 0.3g); PROTEIN 3.2g; CARB 3.7g; FIBER 0.1g; CHOL 13mg; IRON 0.1mg; SODIUM 297mg; CALC 37mg

Menu
PointsPlus value
per serving: 3

Fresh Crab Dip

1 ounce toasted baguette slices
PointsPlus value
per serving: 2

Game Plan

1. Combine cream cheese and chili sauce mixtures in separate bowls.

2. Pick shell from crab.

3. Toast bread.

4. Assemble dip.

pictured on page 33

Menu
PointsPlus value
per serving: 7

**Mediterranean
Goat Cheese Spread**

5 melba toast rounds
PointsPlus value
per serving: 1

Easy Sangría Slush

Game Plan

1. Freeze juice cubes for slush the day before.

2. While tomatoes stand:
  • Chop olives.
  • Combine goat cheese mixture.

3. Process drink just before serving.

Mediterranean Goat Cheese Spread

prep: 4 minutes • **cook:** 2 minutes • **other:** 10 minutes

PointsPlus value per serving: 3

¼   cup water
4   sun-dried tomatoes, packed without oil
2   ounces goat cheese (about ¼ cup)
3   tablespoons fat-free sour cream
⅛   teaspoon salt
6   pitted kalamata olives, finely chopped

1. Combine ¼ cup water and tomatoes in a microwave-safe bowl. Microwave at HIGH 1 minute or until water boils. Remove from microwave; cover with plastic wrap, and let stand 10 minutes to soften.
2. While sun-dried tomatoes stand, place goat cheese in a microwave-safe bowl; microwave at HIGH 15 seconds or until soft. Add sour cream and salt, stirring until well blended; fold in olives.
3. Drain tomatoes; finely chop, and fold into goat cheese mixture. Serve immediately, or cover and chill until ready to serve. **Yield:** 4 servings (serving size: 2 tablespoons).

Per serving: CALORIES 101; FAT 6.7g (sat 3.8g, mono 1.0g, poly 0.2g); PROTEIN 5.5g; CARB 4.7g; FIBER 0.6g; CHOL 16mg; IRON 0.6mg; SODIUM 226mg; CALC 146mg

Easy Sangría Slush

prep: 5 minutes • **other:** 8 hours   *PointsPlus* value per serving: 3

3   cups zinfandel or other fruity dry red wine
½   cup orange juice
½   cup pineapple juice
1   cup sparkling water or club soda
⅓   cup thawed lemonade concentrate

1. Combine first 3 ingredients in a 4-cup glass measure. Pour into ice cube trays. Freeze overnight or until firm.
2. Add frozen juice cubes to food processor; process 30 seconds or until coarsely chopped. Add sparkling water and lemonade concentrate; process 1 minute or until smooth. Pour into a pitcher to serve. **Yield:** 10 servings (serving size: ½ cup).

Per serving: CALORIES 93; FAT 0g; PROTEIN 0.2g; CARB 10g; FIBER 0.1g; CHOL 0mg; IRON 0.2mg; SODIUM 6mg; CALC 5mg

pictured on page 34

Tomato-Basil Bruschetta

prep: 7 minutes • **cook:** 5 minutes   *PointsPlus* value per serving: 2

Bruschetta is an appetizer of toasted bread that is usually topped with some type of cheese, vegetable, or herb. Here, fresh basil leaves add beauty and an extra punch of flavor.

18 (¼-inch-thick) slices diagonally cut whole-grain French bread baguette
Cooking spray
⅓ cup light mayonnaise
 3 ounces tub-style light cream cheese, softened (about ⅓ cup)
 1 tablespoon chopped fresh basil
18 (¼-inch-thick) slices diagonally cut plum tomato
      (about 5 large plum tomatoes)
¼ teaspoon freshly ground black pepper
18 basil leaves

1. Preheat oven to 400°.
2. Place baguette slices on a baking sheet; coat slices with cooking spray. Bake at 400° for 5 minutes or until bread is toasted; set aside.
3. Combine mayonnaise, cream cheese, and chopped basil in a small bowl; stir well.
4. Spread 1 teaspoon cheese mixture on each bread slice; top with tomato slices, and sprinkle with pepper. Top each tomato slice with a basil leaf. **Yield:** 18 servings (serving size: 1 bruschetta).

Per serving: CALORIES 61; FAT 2.8g (sat 0.9g, mono 0.1g, poly 0.3g); PROTEIN 1.9g; CARB 7.3g; FIBER 1g; CHOL 4mg; IRON 0.5mg; SODIUM 121mg; CALC 20mg

Menu
PointsPlus value per serving: 2

Tomato-Basil Bruschetta

1 cup apple slices
PointsPlus value per serving: 0

Game Plan

1. While bread is toasting:
  • Prepare cheese mixture.
  • Slice tomatoes.
  • Slice apples.

2. Assemble bruschetta.

Menu

PointsPlus value
per serving: 8

Steak Crostini with Avocado-Horseradish Mayonnaise

Pimm's Cup (page 22)
PointsPlus value
per serving: 6

Game Plan

1. While rub sits on steak:
- Toast bread.
- Process avocado spread.
- Preheat grill.

2. While steak cooks:
- Slice cucumber and apple for Pimm's Cup.
- Mix drink.

3. Assemble crostini.

Steak Crostini with Avocado-Horseradish Mayonnaise

prep: 12 minutes • **cook:** 13 minutes • **other:** 35 minutes

PointsPlus value per serving: 2

¾ teaspoon kosher salt, divided
½ teaspoon dried oregano
½ teaspoon freshly ground black pepper
½ pound flank steak
1 teaspoon fresh lime juice
¾ teaspoon wasabi (Japanese horseradish)
1 ripe peeled avocado, chopped
1 garlic clove, crushed
3 tablespoons fat-free mayonnaise
Cooking spray
12 (½-inch-thick) slices diagonally cut French bread baguette, toasted
Oregano sprigs (optional)

1. Combine ½ teaspoon salt, dried oregano, and pepper in a small bowl; rub over flank steak. Let stand 30 minutes.

2. Combine lime juice and next 3 ingredients in a food processor; process until smooth. Add mayonnaise and ¼ teaspoon salt; pulse until blended.

3. Preheat grill to medium-high heat.

4. Place steak on grill rack coated with cooking spray; cover and grill 8 to 10 minutes or until desired degree of doneness, turning occasionally. Remove steak from grill, and let stand 5 minutes. Cut steak diagonally across grain into thin slices.

5. Place steak slices on toasted baguette slices; top each with 2 teaspoons avocado spread. Reserve remaining spread for another use. Garnish with oregano sprigs, if desired. **Yield:** 12 servings (serving size: 1 baguette slice, about 2 thin steak slices, and 2 teaspoons spread).

Per serving: CALORIES 79; FAT 4.3g (sat 0.9g, mono 2.1g, poly 0.4g); PROTEIN 5.2g; CARB 6.2g; FIBER 0.8g; CHOL 7mg; IRON 0.6mg; SODIUM 216mg; CALC 13mg

Roasted Cajun-Spiced Edamame

prep: 3 minutes • **cook:** 1 hour and 45 minutes • **other:** 20 minutes

PointsPlus value per serving: 2

    1   (16-ounce) package frozen shelled edamame (green soybeans), thawed
    Olive oil–flavored cooking spray
    1   tablespoon Cajun seasoning
    1   teaspoon onion powder
    ¼   teaspoon kosher salt

1. Preheat oven to 300°.
2. Arrange edamame in a single layer on a baking sheet; lightly coat with cooking spray.
3. Combine Cajun seasoning, onion powder, and salt; sprinkle over edamame, and toss to coat. Bake at 300° for 1 hour and 45 minutes, stirring every 30 minutes. Cool completely. Store in an airtight container. **Yield:** 6 servings (serving size: ¼ cup).

Per serving: CALORIES 103; FAT 3.2g (sat 0.5g, mono 1.0g, poly 1.6g); PROTEIN 8.1g; CARB 9.4g; FIBER 4.1g; CHOL 0mg; IRON 1.6mg; SODIUM 379mg; CALC 52mg

Menu
PointsPlus value
per serving: 3

Roasted Cajun-Spiced Edamame

Crisp Citrus Cooler

Game Plan

1. While edamame bakes:
  • Slice lemon and lime for Crisp Citrus Cooler.
  • Refrigerate juice mixture.

2. Strain juice mixture, and add tonic water.

Crisp Citrus Cooler

prep: 6 minutes • **other:** 30 minutes   *PointsPlus* value per serving: 1

    1   medium lemon
    1   large lime
    3   tablespoons "measures-like-sugar" no-calorie sweetener
    1   (6-ounce) can pineapple juice
    1   (1-ounce) package fresh mint leaves, divided
    1½ cups sugar-free tonic water

1. Cut lemon and lime in half crosswise, and squeeze 3 tablespoons juice from each into a large zip-top plastic bag, reserving rinds. Add reserved rinds, sweetener, pineapple juice, and half of mint leaves to bag; seal tightly. Squeeze mixture 15 to 20 seconds or until oils from rinds are released and mint leaves are bruised. Refrigerate 30 minutes.
2. Strain mixture through a fine sieve over a pitcher, squeezing rinds to extract remaining juice. Discard strained fruit and mint; gently stir in tonic water.
3. Fill 5 tall glasses three-fourths full with crushed ice. Top ice with remaining mint leaves, and pour juice mixture into glasses. Serve immediately. **Yield:** 5 servings (serving size: about ½ cup).

Per serving: CALORIES 29; FAT 0.1g; PROTEIN 0.3g; CARB 7.4g; FIBER 0.2g; CHOL 0mg; IRON 0.3mg; SODIUM 12mg; CALC 9mg

Menu

PointsPlus value
per serving: 3

Sweet and Spicy Snack Mix

1 cup light lemonade
PointsPlus value
per serving: 0

Game Plan

1. While oven preheats:
- Pop popcorn.
- Measure and combine
  popcorn, cereals, pretzels,
  and raisins.
- Line baking sheet with
  foil.
- Combine melted butter
  mixture.

2. Serve lemonade over ice
with snack mix once cool.

Sweet and Spicy Snack Mix

prep: 7 minutes • **cook:** 17 minutes   *PointsPlus* value per serving: 3

This mix cures your sweet and salty craving in one bite. We tested with a 10-ounce package of low-fat microwave popcorn and used about half the bag in this recipe.

    5   cups popped low-fat microwave popcorn
    2   cups multigrain cereal squares
    2   cups multigrain toasted oat cereal
    1   cup butter-flavored pretzels
    ½   cup raisins
    2   tablespoons unsalted butter, melted
    1   tablespoon chili powder
    2   tablespoons honey
    Dash of ground red pepper (optional)

1. Preheat oven to 350°.
2. Combine first 5 ingredients in a large bowl. Combine melted butter, chili powder, honey, and, if desired, ground red pepper, stirring well. Pour butter mixture over popcorn mixture, and stir to combine.
3. Spread mixture on a baking sheet lined with foil. Bake at 350° for 15 minutes. Cool and store in an airtight container. **Yield:** 11 servings (serving size: 1 cup).

Per serving: CALORIES 120; FAT 2.7g (sat 1.4g, mono 0.7g, poly 0.3g); PROTEIN 2g; CARB 24.1g; FIBER 1.7g; CHOL 5mg; IRON 4.8mg; SODIUM 200mg; CALC 22mg

Fresh Figs Topped with Goat Cheese and Honey

prep: 10 minutes • **cook:** 4 minutes • **other:** 5 minutes

PointsPlus value per serving: 4

A variety of flavored honey is available in supermarkets. The most common types are clover and orange blossom. We tested with summer flowers honey, but use whatever you prefer.

- 8 fresh figs
- 2 teaspoons balsamic vinegar
- 2 ounces crumbled goat cheese (about ½ cup)
- 2 tablespoons flavored honey
- 1 tablespoon minced fresh mint

1. Preheat broiler.

2. Cut figs in half lengthwise. Arrange figs on a baking sheet, cut sides up, and brush with balsamic vinegar. Broil 4 minutes or until thoroughly heated. Place figs on a serving platter; cool 5 minutes.

3. Top each fig half with 1½ teaspoons goat cheese; drizzle with honey, and sprinkle with mint. **Yield:** 16 servings (serving size: 1 fig half).

Per serving: CALORIES 131; FAT 1.4g (sat 0.9g, mono 0.3g, poly 0.1g); PROTEIN 1.9g; CARB 30.9g; FIBER 2.1g; CHOL 3mg; IRON 0.6mg; SODIUM 22mg; CALC 14mg

Menu

PointsPlus value per serving: 8

Fresh Figs Topped with Goat Cheese and Honey

5 ounces white wine
PointsPlus value per serving: 4

Game Plan

1. While broiler preheats:
- Cut figs.
- Brush figs with vinegar.

2. While figs broil:
- Crumble cheese.
- Mince mint.

3. Top fig halves, and serve with chilled wine.

Pickled Shrimp

prep: 5 minutes • **other:** 24 hours   *PointsPlus* value per serving: 3

- 1 large lemon
- 1½ cups water
- ½ cup light olive oil vinaigrette
- 1 teaspoon pickling spice
- 1 pound cooked peeled medium shrimp
- 1 medium-sized red onion, thinly sliced

1. Thinly slice half of lemon; set aside. Squeeze remaining half of lemon over a small bowl to measure 2 tablespoons juice; add 1½ cups water, vinaigrette, and pickling spice.

2. Layer shrimp, onion, and lemon slices in a shallow dish or wide-mouthed jar. Pour lemon juice mixture over layers. Cover and refrigerate at least 24 hours. **Yield:** 8 servings (serving size: about 7 shrimp and ¼ cup onion).

Per serving: CALORIES 103; FAT 3.6g (sat 0.6g, mono 0.6g, poly 1.3g); PROTEIN 14.3g; CARB 3g; FIBER 0.2g; CHOL 115mg; IRON 1.2mg; SODIUM 283mg; CALC 44mg

Menu

PointsPlus value per serving: 6

Pickled Shrimp

1 ounce baked pita chips
PointsPlus value per serving: 3

Game Plan

1. Cook and peel shrimp.

2. Slice lemon and onion.

3. Refrigerate shrimp mixture overnight.

4. Serve chilled with pita chips.

Menu

PointsPlus value
per serving: 2

Marinated Tortellini

1 cup grapes
PointsPlus value
per serving: 0

Game Plan

1. While pasta cooks:
 • Chop basil, and mince garlic.

2. Marinate at least 4 hours.

3. Serve chilled or at room temperature with grapes.

Marinated Tortellini

prep: 6 minutes • **cook:** 13 minutes • **other:** 4 hours

PointsPlus value per serving: 2

You can make this appetizer up to a day before you plan to serve it. When it marinates overnight, it has more flavor. Triple the serving size for a hearty meatless lunch with a *PointsPlus* value of 7.

    1 (9-ounce) package fresh three-cheese tortellini
    1 (9-ounce) package fresh mozzarella-garlic tortellini
 1½ cups grape tomatoes
   ⅓ cup chopped fresh basil
   ½ cup light balsamic vinaigrette
   ⅓ cup water
    1 tablespoon brown sugar
    1 large garlic clove, minced

1. Cook pasta according to package directions, omitting salt and fat. Drain and rinse with cold water; drain. Combine pasta, tomatoes, and basil in a large bowl.
2. Combine vinaigrette and next 3 ingredients in a small bowl; stir well with a whisk. Pour marinade over pasta; toss gently. Cover and marinate in refrigerator at least 4 hours. **Yield:** 21 servings (serving size: ⅓ cup).

Per serving: CALORIES 87; FAT 2.8g (sat 1.2g, mono 0g, poly 0g); PROTEIN 3.6g; CARB 12g; FIBER 0.6g; CHOL 11mg; IRON 0.3mg; SODIUM 184mg; CALC 33mg

Taco Cups

prep: 13 minutes • **cook:** 20 minutes   *PointsPlus* value per serving: 1

A 2.1-ounce package of mini phyllo shells contains 15 shells, so you'll need to buy two packages. Store the remaining shells in an airtight container in the refrigerator or freezer for another use.

½   pound ground sirloin
2   tablespoons 40%-less-sodium taco seasoning
¾   cup bottled salsa, divided
2   tablespoons canned chopped green chiles
24   mini phyllo shells
2   ounces reduced-fat shredded Monterey Jack cheese (about ½ cup)
¼   cup fat-free sour cream

1. Preheat oven to 350°.
2. Cook beef and taco seasoning in a large skillet over medium-high heat until beef is browned, stirring to crumble. Drain, if necessary; return to pan. Add ½ cup salsa and chiles; stir.
3. Fill phyllo shells with meat mixture. Top with cheese. Bake at 350° for 10 minutes or until thoroughly heated and cheese melts. Remove from oven, and top each taco cup with ½ teaspoon each of salsa and sour cream. **Yield:** 24 servings (serving size: 1 taco cup).

Per serving: CALORIES 48; FAT 2.4g (sat 0.6g, mono 1.0g, poly 0.2g); PROTEIN 2.8g; CARB 3g; FIBER 0.1g; CHOL 8mg; IRON 0.4mg; SODIUM 128mg; CALC 30mg

Menu
PointsPlus value per serving: 4

Taco Cups

Frozen Blueberry-Lime Margaritas (page 22)
PointsPlus value per serving: 3

Game Plan

1. Cook taco filling in skillet.

2. Fill phyllo shells, and top with cheese.

3. While Taco Cups bake:
• Grate lime rind, and squeeze juice for margaritas.
• Combine margarita ingredients in blender.

4. Process margarita just before ready to serve.

Menu
PointsPlus value
per serving: 7

Mini Greek Chicken Salad Bites

**Pomegranate Martinis
(page 23)**
PointsPlus value
per serving: 6

Game Plan

1. While chicken cools:
- Chop olives and dill, and dice onions.
- Cut orange rind strips.

2. Prepare salad mixture.

3. Just before serving:
- Spoon salad mixture into shells.
- Shake martinis.

Mini Greek Chicken Salad Bites

prep: 19 minutes • **cook:** 23 minutes   *PointsPlus* value per serving: 1

If you're planning to prepare this appetizer more than a couple of hours ahead, chill the chicken salad by itself, and hold off on filling the shells. After a few hours, the shells can become soggy.

  2 (6-ounce) skinless, boneless chicken breast halves
  3 ounces crumbled feta cheese (about ¾ cup)
  ½ cup light mayonnaise
  ¼ cup sliced ripe olives, chopped
  ¼ cup diced red onion
  1 tablespoon chopped fresh dill or 1 teaspoon dried dill
  ¼ teaspoon freshly ground black pepper
  ⅛ teaspoon salt
  3 (2.1-ounce) packages mini phyllo shells
Fresh dill sprigs (optional)

1. Place chicken in a saucepan; add water to cover. Bring to a boil; reduce heat, and simmer 18 minutes or until chicken is done. Remove from pan; let cool. Place chicken in a food processor. Pulse 3 to 5 times or until chicken is finely chopped.

2. Combine chicken, cheese, and next 6 ingredients in a bowl; stir until combined. Spoon about 1 tablespoon chicken mixture into each phyllo shell. Serve immediately, or cover and chill up to 2 hours. Garnish with dill sprigs, if desired. Yield: 45 servings (serving size: 1 stuffed phyllo shell).

Per serving: CALORIES 42; FAT 2.6g (sat 0.6g, mono 0.7g, poly 0.2g); PROTEIN 2.1g; CARB 2.4g; FIBER 0g; CHOL 8mg; IRON 0.3mg; SODIUM 80mg; CALC 14mg

Chicken Tenders with Pita Coating

prep: 8 minutes • **cook:** 15 minutes   *PointsPlus* value per serving: 2

- ½ cup egg substitute
- ½ teaspoon freshly ground black pepper
- 1½ cups Parmesan, garlic, and herb–flavored pita chips, finely crushed
- 1 tablespoon salt-free Italian seasoning
- 8 (2-ounce) chicken breast tenders
- Cooking spray
- ½ cup tomato-basil pasta sauce, warmed

1. Preheat oven to 400°.
2. Heat a large baking sheet in oven 5 minutes.
3. Combine egg substitute and pepper in a shallow dish. Combine chips and Italian seasoning in another shallow dish. Dip chicken in egg mixture; dredge in chip mixture. Coat preheated baking sheet with cooking spray, and place chicken on pan.
4. Bake at 400° for 15 minutes or until done. Serve with pasta sauce. **Yield:** 8 servings (serving size: 1 chicken breast tender and 1 tablespoon pasta sauce).

Per serving: CALORIES 92; FAT 2.2g (sat 0.4g, mono 0.5g, poly 0.3g); PROTEIN 13.6g; CARB 3.4g; FIBER 0.4g; CHOL 31mg; IRON 0.9mg; SODIUM 116mg; CALC 18mg

---

Menu
PointsPlus value
per serving: 5

**Chicken Tenders
with Pita Coating**

**White
Cranberry–Peach
Spritzer**

Game Plan

1. While oven preheats:
- Crush pita chips.
- Prepare egg mixture and chip mixture.

2. Dip and dredge chicken in egg and chip mixtures.

3. While chicken bakes:
- Slice peaches and lime for spritzer.
- Warm pasta sauce.
- Prepare spritzer.

White Cranberry–Peach Spritzer

prep: 2 minutes   *PointsPlus* value per serving: 3

Sparkling water and sliced peaches add oomph to simple juice. Use crushed ice for an especially refreshing treat.

- 2 cups white cranberry–peach juice
- ⅔ cup peach nectar
- ⅔ cup sparkling water
- ½ cup fresh or frozen sliced peaches
- 4 lime wedges

1. Combine first 3 ingredients in a 1-quart pitcher; stir gently. Pour about ¾ cup juice mixture into each of 4 tall glasses. Divide peach slices among glasses, and squeeze a lime wedge into each glass. Fill glasses with ice. Serve immediately. **Yield:** 4 servings (serving size: ¾ cup juice mixture with fruit).

Per serving: CALORIES 91; FAT 0g; PROTEIN 0.3g; CARB 23.5g; FIBER 0.4g; CHOL 0mg; IRON 0.1mg; SODIUM 21mg; CALC 3mg

Menu
PointsPlus value
per serving: 2

Sausage-Stuffed Red Potatoes

1 cup baby carrots
PointsPlus value
per serving: 0

**2 tablespoons fat-free
ranch dressing**
PointsPlus value
per serving: 1

Game Plan

1. Chop produce.

2. While potatoes cook:
• Prepare sausage mixture.

3. Scoop out pulp, and stuff
potato halves.

4. Serve potato halves warm.

Sausage-Stuffed Red Potatoes

prep: 13 minutes • **cook:** 10 minutes   *PointsPlus* value per serving: 1

8   small red potatoes (about 1½ pounds)
Cooking spray
1   (4-ounce) link turkey Italian sausage, casing removed
½   red bell pepper, finely chopped (about ¾ cup)
¼   cup finely chopped green onions
2   tablespoons chopped fresh parsley
2   ounces reduced-fat shredded extra-sharp cheddar cheese (about ½ cup)
⅛   teaspoon salt

1. Pierce potatoes with a fork; arrange on paper towels in a microwave oven. Microwave at HIGH 8 minutes or until tender.

2. While potatoes cook, heat a large nonstick skillet over medium-high heat; coat pan with cooking spray. Add sausage to pan; cook 4 minutes or until browned, stirring to crumble. Add bell pepper, and cook 2 minutes. Add onions and parsley; cook 30 seconds, and remove from heat. Sprinkle cheese over sausage mixture, and toss gently to blend.

3. Cut potatoes in half lengthwise, and carefully scoop out 1 teaspoon potato pulp from each half, leaving shells intact. Discard potato pulp. Sprinkle potato halves with salt. Spoon 1 tablespoon sausage mixture onto each potato half; microwave at HIGH 2 minutes or until cheese melts. Serve warm. **Yield:** 16 servings (serving size: 1 stuffed potato half).

Per serving: CALORIES 47; FAT 1.6g (sat 0.8g, mono 0g, poly 0g); PROTEIN 3g; CARB 5.3g; FIBER 0.7g; CHOL 9mg; IRON 0.4mg; SODIUM 77mg; CALC 32mg

Sweet Potato Fries with Maple-Ginger Dip

prep: 10 minutes • **cook:** 30 minutes   *PointsPlus* value per serving: 3

3 sweet potatoes (about 1½ pounds), cut into ½-inch-wide strips
Olive oil–flavored cooking spray
½ teaspoon salt
½ cup light sour cream
1 tablespoon maple syrup
½ teaspoon grated peeled fresh ginger

1. Preheat oven to 450°.
2. Place potatoes in a single layer on a large shallow metal baking pan coated with cooking spray. Sprinkle potatoes with salt. Bake at 450° for 30 minutes, turning once.
3. While potatoes cook, combine sour cream, syrup, and ginger in a small bowl. Serve potatoes immediately with dip. **Yield:** 6 servings (serving size: ½ cup fries and about 1½ tablespoons dip).

Per serving: CALORIES 106; FAT 2.5g (sat 1.5g, mono 0.7g, poly 0.1g); PROTEIN 1.9g; CARB 19.6g; FIBER 2.5g; CHOL 8mg; IRON 0.6mg; SODIUM 247mg; CALC 48mg

Menu
PointsPlus value per serving: 6

Sweet Potato Fries with Maple-Ginger Dip

Iced Green Tea–Citrus Punch

Game Plan
1. Prepare punch and chill.
2. Cut sweet potatoes.
3. While potatoes cook:
• Grate ginger.
• Make dip for fries.

Iced Green Tea–Citrus Punch

prep: 2 minutes • **cook:** 6 minutes • **other:** 1 hour and 35 minutes

PointsPlus value per serving: 3

6 cups water, divided
1 cup sugar
16 green tea bags
1¾ cups fresh orange juice (about 6 large oranges)
¼ cup fresh lemon juice (about 3 lemons)
Orange slices (optional)

1. Bring 3 cups water and sugar to a boil in a large saucepan, stirring until sugar dissolves. Remove pan from heat; add tea bags, and steep 5 minutes. Remove tea bags with a slotted spoon (do not squeeze).
2. Cool tea to room temperature; stir in orange juice, lemon juice, and 3 cups water. Cover and chill at least 1 hour. Serve over ice; garnish with orange slices, if desired. **Yield:** 8 servings (serving size: 1 cup).

Per serving: CALORIES 123; FAT 0g; PROTEIN 0.4g; CARB 31.3g; FIBER 0.1g; CHOL 0mg; IRON 0.1mg; SODIUM 1mg; CALC 7mg

pictured on page 35

Frozen Blueberry-Lime Margaritas

Menu
PointsPlus value per serving: 4

Frozen Blueberry-Lime Margaritas

Taco Cups (page 17)
PointsPlus value per serving: 1

Game Plan

1. Cook taco filling in skillet.

2. Fill phyllo shells, and top with cheese.

3. While Taco Cups bake:
- Grate lime rind, and squeeze juice.
- Combine margarita ingredients in blender.

4. Process margarita just before ready to serve.

prep: 13 minutes

PointsPlus value per serving: 3

You can prepare this margarita mix ahead, and freeze it in a freezer-safe container. Just before serving, thaw it slightly and scrape with a fork.

> 3 cups crushed ice
> 2¾ cups frozen blueberries
> 1 cup cold water
> ¾ cup "measures-like-sugar" no-calorie sweetener
> 2 teaspoons grated fresh lime rind
> ½ cup fresh lime juice (about 5 limes)
> ¼ cup orange-flavored liqueur
> ¼ cup tequila
> Lime slices (optional)

1. Combine first 8 ingredients in a blender; process until smooth. Serve immediately. Garnish with lime slices, if desired. **Yield:** 5 servings (serving size: 1 cup).

Per serving: CALORIES 68; FAT 0.3g; PROTEIN 0.3g; CARB 9g; FIBER 1.3g; CHOL 0mg; IRON 0.1mg; SODIUM 1mg; CALC 6mg

Pimm's Cup

Menu
PointsPlus value per serving: 8

Pimm's Cup

Steak Crostini with Avocado-Horseradish Mayonnaise (page 12)
PointsPlus value per serving: 2

Game Plan

1. While rub sits on steak:
- Toast bread.
- Process avocado spread.
- Preheat grill.

2. While steak cooks:
- Slice cucumber and apple for Pimm's Cup.
- Mix drink.

3. Assemble crostini.

prep: 5 minutes

PointsPlus value per serving: 6

Pimm's No. 1 is a gin-based liquor that's as much a part of British culture as a cup of tea. The golden-brown liquor tastes like citrus fruits and spices. It's either served on the rocks or used in cocktails like this one.

> 18 (¼-inch-thick) slices English cucumber
> 3 medium Granny Smith apples (about 1 pound), cored and quartered
> 1½ cups Pimm's No. 1
> 3 cups light lemonade

1. Place 3 cucumber slices and 2 apple wedges in each of 6 tall glasses. Add ¼ cup Pimm's No. 1 to each glass; let stand 1 minute. Fill glasses with ice; add ½ cup lemonade to each glass. Stir and serve immediately. **Yield:** 6 servings (serving size: 1 drink).

Per serving: CALORIES 178; FAT 0g; PROTEIN 0.4g; CARB 10.4g; FIBER 1.5g; CHOL 0mg; IRON 0.2mg; SODIUM 4mg; CALC 7mg

Ginger-Lime Martinis

prep: 27 minutes • **cook:** 18 minutes • **other:** 1 hour

PointsPlus value per serving: 7

  1   cup chopped peeled fresh ginger (1 large root)
  ¾   cup sugar
1½ cups water
  2   cups vodka, chilled and divided
  ¼   cup fresh lime juice, divided (about 2½ limes)
      Lime wedges (optional)
      Mint leaves (optional)

1. Combine first 3 ingredients in a small saucepan; bring to a boil. Reduce heat; simmer, uncovered, 15 minutes, stirring occasionally. Strain mixture through a sieve into a bowl; discard solids. Chill ginger syrup 1 hour or until very cold.
2. Fill a martini shaker with ice. Add ¼ cup chilled ginger syrup, ½ cup chilled vodka, and 1 tablespoon lime juice. Shake well; strain into 2 martini glasses. Repeat procedure 3 times with remaining ginger syrup, vodka, and lime juice. Garnish glasses with lime wedges and mint leaves, if desired. **Yield:** 8 servings (serving size: 1 martini).

Per serving: CALORIES 248; FAT 0.1g; PROTEIN 0.3g; CARB 21.5g; FIBER 0.3g; CHOL 0mg; IRON 0.1mg; SODIUM 2mg; CALC 3mg

---

Menu
PointsPlus value per serving: 9

Ginger-Lime Martinis

1 cup mixed vegetables
PointsPlus value per serving: 0

3 tablespoons spinach-artichoke hummus
PointsPlus value per serving: 2

Game Plan

1. Prepare and chill ginger syrup.

2. Chop vegetables.

3. Squeeze limes.

4. Combine and shake martini ingredients.

Pomegranate Martinis

prep: 5 minutes   *PointsPlus* value per serving: 6

If you happen to have lemon- or orange-flavored vodka on hand, use it as a flavorful alternative to plain vodka.

  1   cup crushed ice
  ½   cup pomegranate juice
  6   tablespoons chilled vodka
  3   tablespoons orange-flavored liqueur
  1   tablespoon fresh lemon juice
  2   (2-inch) orange rind strips

1. Place crushed ice in a martini shaker. Add pomegranate juice and next 3 ingredients. Shake well; strain into 2 martini glasses.
2. Rub rim of each martini glass with inside of orange rind. Twist rind; drop into glasses. Serve immediately. **Yield:** 2 servings (serving size: about ⅔ cup).

Per serving: CALORIES 213; FAT 0g; PROTEIN 0.3g; CARB 16.6g; FIBER 0g; CHOL 0mg; IRON 0.1mg; SODIUM 8mg; CALC 11mg

---

Menu
PointsPlus value per serving: 7

Pomegranate Martinis

Mini Greek Chicken Salad Bites (page 18)
PointsPlus value per serving: 1

Game Plan

1. While chicken cools:
• Chop olives, onion, and dill.
• Cut orange rind strips.

2. Prepare salad mixture.

3. Just before serving:
• Spoon salad mixture into shells.
• Shake martinis.

Triple-Fruit Soy Smoothies

prep: 4 minutes • **other:** 30 minutes   *PointsPlus* value per serving: 4

If you're in a hurry, you can skip the first step of freezing the fruit. The smoothies won't be quite as thick and frosty, but the flavor will still be great.

    3   cups strawberries, halved
    2   medium bananas, sliced into 1-inch pieces
    1   cup vanilla soy milk
    ½   cup orange juice
    ⅓   cup "measures-like-sugar" no-calorie sweetener

1. Place strawberries and banana slices on a foil-lined jelly-roll pan. Freeze 30 minutes.
2. Place frozen fruit, soy milk, orange juice, and sweetener in a blender; process until smooth. **Yield:** 4 servings (serving size: 1 cup).

Per serving: CALORIES 154; FAT 1.4g (sat 0.2g, mono 0.1g, poly 0.2g); PROTEIN 3.3g; CARB 34.7g; FIBER 4.6g; CHOL 0mg; IRON 1.2mg; SODIUM 36mg; CALC 97mg

Menu
PointsPlus value
per serving: 6

Triple-Fruit Soy Smoothies

2 cups light
microwave popcorn
PointsPlus value
per serving: 2

Game Plan

1. Freeze fruit.

2. While popcorn pops:
• Combine smoothie
  ingredients in blender.

3. Process smoothie.

Spiced Mocha Latte

prep: 2 minutes • **cook:** 2 minutes   *PointsPlus* value per serving: 2

The drinks at the local coffee shop can be loaded with calories. This homemade version is not, and you can prepare it in five minutes. It's just the thing to perk you up in the afternoon, and it's a good source of calcium.

    ⅔   cup hot strong brewed coffee
    1   (0.55-ounce) envelope no-sugar-added instant cocoa mix
    ⅓   cup fat-free milk
    ¼   teaspoon "measures-like-sugar" no-calorie sweetener
    ⅛   teaspoon ground cinnamon
    1   tablespoon frozen fat-free whipped topping, thawed
    Unsweetened cocoa (optional)

1. Combine coffee and cocoa mix in a large mug, stirring until blended.
2. Microwave milk at HIGH 30 seconds or until hot; stir into cocoa mixture. Add sweetener and cinnamon; stir until blended. Top with whipped topping. Dust with cocoa, if desired. Serve immediately. **Yield:** 1 serving (serving size: 1 cup).

Per serving: CALORIES 95; FAT 0.6g (sat 0.3g, mono 0.2g, poly 0g); PROTEIN 7.4g; CARB 14.7g; FIBER 0.9g; CHOL 5mg; IRON 0.6mg; SODIUM 188mg; CALC 237mg

Menu
PointsPlus value
per serving: 5

Spiced Mocha Latte

4 vanilla wafer cookies
PointsPlus value
per serving: 3

Game Plan

1. While coffee brews:
• Thaw whipped topping.
• Heat milk.

2. Prepare latte.

3. Serve hot with cookies.

Breakfast

Menu
PointsPlus value
per serving: 5

Pumpkin Streusel Muffins

1 cup strawberries and grapes
PointsPlus value
per serving: 0

Game Plan

1. While oven preheats:
• Prepare muffin mixture.

2. While muffins bake:
• Cut up fruit.

Pumpkin Streusel Muffins

prep: 18 minutes • **cook:** 22 minutes • **other:** 5 minutes

PointsPlus value per serving: 5

A crunchy streusel tops these moist spiced muffins.

⅓ cup quick-cooking oats
2 tablespoons brown sugar
2 tablespoons all-purpose flour
1½ tablespoons light stick butter, melted
9 ounces self-rising flour (about 2 cups)
1 cup quick-cooking oats
¾ cup packed brown sugar
2 teaspoons pumpkin pie spice
¼ teaspoon salt
½ cup 1% low-fat milk
¼ cup canola oil
1 (15-ounce) can pumpkin
1 large egg, lightly beaten
Cooking spray

1. Preheat oven to 400°.

2. Combine first 4 ingredients, stirring until dry ingredients are moistened and mixture holds together; set aside.

3. Weigh or lightly spoon self-rising flour into dry measuring cups; level with a knife. Combine 2 cups flour and next 4 ingredients in a large bowl; make a well in center of mixture. Combine milk and next 3 ingredients; stir with a whisk. Add to flour mixture, stirring just until moist.

4. Spoon batter into 16 muffin cups coated with cooking spray. Sprinkle with streusel mixture.

5. Bake at 400° for 22 to 25 minutes or until golden. Cool muffins in pan on a wire rack 5 minutes; remove from pans, and place on wire rack. Serve warm.
Yield: 16 muffins (serving size: 1 muffin).

Per serving: CALORIES 181; FAT 5.2g (sat 0.9g, mono 2.5g, poly 1.3g); PROTEIN 3.6g; CARB 30.9g; FIBER 1.9g; CHOL 15mg; IRON 1.8mg; SODIUM 259mg; CALC 87mg

Peanut Butter–Chocolate Chip Scones

prep: 16 minutes • **cook:** 14 minutes   *PointsPlus* value per serving: 5

Combine peanut butter and chocolate for a rich breakfast treat. Natural peanut butter with no added sugars boasts the best peanut flavor and contains no trans fats.

  7.9 ounces all-purpose flour (about 1¾ cups)
   ⅓ cup packed brown sugar
  2½ teaspoons baking powder
   ¼ teaspoon salt
   2 tablespoons chilled butter, cut into small pieces
   ½ cup natural-style chunky peanut butter
   ½ cup fat-free milk
   1 teaspoon vanilla extract
   1 large egg, lightly beaten
   ¼ cup semisweet chocolate minichips
  Cooking spray

1. Preheat oven to 425°.

2. Weigh or lightly spoon flour into dry measuring cups; level with a knife. Combine flour and next 3 ingredients in a large bowl; cut in butter with a pastry blender or 2 knives until mixture resembles coarse meal.

3. Combine peanut butter and next 3 ingredients, stirring with a whisk. Add to flour mixture, stirring just until moist. Stir in chocolate chips. Knead dough 4 times in bowl.

4. Pat dough into a 7-inch circle on a baking sheet coated with cooking spray. Cut dough into 12 wedges, cutting into but not through dough (do not separate wedges). Lightly coat with cooking spray.

5. Bake at 425° for 14 minutes or until lightly browned. **Yield:** 12 servings (serving size: 1 scone).

Per serving: CALORIES 201; FAT 8.9g (sat 2.9g, mono 1g, poly 0.2g); PROTEIN 5.3g; CARB 25.1g; FIBER 1.4g; CHOL 23mg; IRON 1.4mg; SODIUM 159mg; CALC 75mg

Menu
PointsPlus value per serving: 7

Peanut Butter–Chocolate Chip Scones

1 cup fat-free milk
PointsPlus value per serving: 2

Game Plan

1. While oven preheats:
  • Combine scone mixture.
  • Coat baking sheet with cooking spray.

2. Bake scones.

3. Serve scones warm with cold milk.

Menu
PointsPlus value
per serving: 5

Banana–Macadamia
Nut Pancakes

2 tablespoons
light maple-flavored syrup
PointsPlus value
per serving: 1

Game Plan

1. Chop banana and nuts, and toast nuts.

2. While griddle heats:
   • Combine pancake mixture.

3. While pancakes cook:
   • Warm syrup.

Banana–Macadamia Nut Pancakes

prep: 6 minutes • **cook:** 3 minutes per batch   *PointsPlus* value per serving: 4

Chopped macadamia nuts add a bit of crunch to these sweet banana pancakes. Serve with light maple syrup, if desired.

  5.6 ounces all-purpose flour (about 1¼ cups)
  1½ teaspoons baking powder
  ½ teaspoon baking soda
  ½ teaspoon salt
  1 cup chopped ripe banana (about 2 small)
  1 cup low-fat buttermilk
  3 tablespoons brown sugar
  1 tablespoon butter, softened
  1 teaspoon vanilla extract
  1 large egg
  ⅓ cup chopped macadamia nuts, toasted
  Cooking spray

1. Weigh or lightly spoon flour into dry measuring cups; level with a knife. Combine flour and next 3 ingredients in a large bowl; stir with a whisk. Combine banana and next 5 ingredients in a medium bowl; stir with a whisk until smooth. Add buttermilk mixture to flour mixture; stir just until combined. Stir in macadamia nuts.

2. Pour about ¼ cup batter per pancake onto a hot nonstick griddle or nonstick skillet coated with cooking spray. Cook 1 to 2 minutes or until tops are covered with bubbles and edges look cooked. Carefully turn pancakes over, and cook 1 to 2 minutes or until bottoms are lightly browned. Repeat with remaining batter.
Yield: 11 servings (serving size: 1 pancake).

Per serving: CALORIES 133; FAT 5g (sat 1.4g, mono 2.9g, poly 0.2g); PROTEIN 3.3g; CARB 19.1g; FIBER 1.2g; CHOL 23mg; IRON 1mg; SODIUM 258mg; CALC 69mg

Flaxseed Pancakes with Honey

prep: 5 minutes • **cook:** 3 minutes per batch   *PointsPlus* value per serving: 6

Flaxseed is high in both fiber and omega-3 fatty acids. Be sure to store it in the refrigerator after opening for maximum freshness.

- 4.5 ounces all-purpose flour (about 1 cup)
- ¼ cup flaxseed meal
- 1 teaspoon baking powder
- ½ teaspoon baking soda
- ¼ teaspoon salt
- 1 cup nonfat buttermilk
- 2 teaspoons canola oil
- 1 large egg
- Cooking spray
- 2 tablespoons honey

1. Weigh or lightly spoon flour into a dry measuring cup; level with a knife. Combine flour and next 4 ingredients in a large bowl, stirring with a whisk.
2. Combine buttermilk, oil, and egg, stirring with a whisk until blended; add to flour mixture, stirring just until dry ingredients are moist.
3. Pour about ¼ cup batter per pancake onto a hot nonstick griddle or nonstick skillet coated with cooking spray. Cook 1½ minutes or until tops are covered with bubbles and edges look cooked. Carefully turn pancakes over; cook 1½ minutes or until bottoms are lightly browned. Repeat procedure with remaining batter.
4. Place honey in a small bowl. Microwave at HIGH 20 seconds or just until warm. Drizzle each serving with honey. **Yield:** 4 servings (serving size: 2 pancakes and 1½ teaspoons honey).

Per serving: CALORIES 242; FAT 6.1g (sat 0.9g, mono 2.5g, poly 2.7g); PROTEIN 8.6g; CARB 38.6g; FIBER 2.8g; CHOL 53mg; IRON 2mg; SODIUM 520mg; CALC 46mg

Menu
PointsPlus value per serving: 6

Flaxseed Pancakes with Honey

1 cup blueberries
PointsPlus value per serving: 0

Game Plan

1. While griddle heats:
- Combine pancake mixture.

2. While pancakes cook:
- Warm honey.
- Measure blueberries.

Menu
PointsPlus value
per serving: 9

Peaches-and-Cream
French Toast

1 cup light orange juice
PointsPlus value
per serving: 1

Game Plan

1. While pan heats:
- Spread cream cheese mixture over bread slices.
- Whisk egg substitute mixture.

2. Dip sandwiches in egg mixture, and cook.

3. Warm syrup and drizzle over toast.

Peaches-and-Cream French Toast

prep: 5 minutes • **cook:** 4 minutes per batch   *PointsPlus* value per serving: 8

This French toast brings the flavors of summer to a cold winter's day. For additional flavor, use drained and chopped canned peaches in place of peach preserves.

- 4 ounces ⅓-less-fat cream cheese, softened (about ½ cup)
- ¼ cup low-sugar peach preserves
- 8 (1-ounce) slices whole-grain white bread
- 1 cup egg substitute
- ½ cup fat-free half-and-half
- ½ teaspoon vanilla extract
- Butter-flavored cooking spray
- ¼ cup light maple-flavored syrup
- 4 teaspoons powdered sugar (optional)

1. Combine cream cheese and preserves in a small bowl. Spread cream cheese mixture over 4 bread slices; top with remaining bread slices.

2. Combine egg substitute, half-and-half, and vanilla in a shallow dish, stirring with a whisk. Heat a large nonstick griddle or nonstick skillet over medium heat. Coat pan with cooking spray. Dip 2 sandwiches in egg mixture on both sides, and place in pan. Cook 2 minutes on each side or until browned. Repeat with remaining 2 sandwiches. Drizzle each serving with 1 tablespoon syrup. Sprinkle with powdered sugar, if desired. **Yield:** 4 servings (serving size: 1 stuffed toast and 1 tablespoon syrup).

Per serving: CALORIES 318; FAT 8.5g (sat 4.1g, mono 1.6g, poly 1.3g); PROTEIN 14.6g; CARB 45.6g; FIBER 3g; CHOL 21mg; IRON 2.9mg; SODIUM 451mg; CALC 502mg

Pineapple-Stuffed French Toast

prep: 11 minutes • **cook:** 7 minutes   *PointsPlus* value per serving: 4

You'll need five slices of French bread for this recipe; use what's left from the loaf to make sandwiches at lunch or for your evening meal.

  2   ounces honey-nut tub-style cream cheese (about ¼ cup)
  1   (8-ounce) can crushed pineapple in juice, drained
  5   (6-inch-long) slices presliced French bread
1½   cups egg substitute
      Cooking spray
      Light maple-flavored syrup (optional)

1. Preheat oven to 400°.
2. Combine cream cheese and pineapple. Cut a horizontal slit through 1 side of each bread slice to form a deep pocket. Stuff about 2 tablespoons pineapple mixture into each pocket, pressing down gently.
3. Pour egg substitute into a shallow bowl. Heat a large nonstick skillet over medium heat. Coat pan with cooking spray. Dip stuffed bread slices in egg substitute. Add bread to pan; cook 2 minutes on each side or until lightly browned. Place browned toasts on a baking sheet coated with cooking spray.
4. Bake at 400° for 3 minutes or until egg mixture on sides of toasts is cooked. Top with syrup, if desired. **Yield:** 5 servings (serving size: 1 piece).

Per serving: CALORIES 166; FAT 3.4g (sat 1.7g, mono 0.8g, poly 0.3g); PROTEIN 11g; CARB 23.5g; FIBER 0.9g; CHOL 11mg; IRON 2.5mg; SODIUM 372mg; CALC 76mg

Menu
PointsPlus value
per serving: 7

Pineapple-Stuffed French Toast

2 tablespoons light maple-flavored syrup
PointsPlus value
per serving: 1

3 slices turkey bacon
PointsPlus value
per serving: 2

Game Plan

1. Stuff bread pockets.

2. While oven preheats:
  • Heat skillet.
  • Whisk egg substitute mixture.

3. While toast cooks:
  • Microwave bacon until crisp.

Menu

PointsPlus value
per serving: 8

**Individual Apple-Walnut
Coffee Cakes**

1 cup fat-free milk
PointsPlus value
per serving: 2

Game Plan

1. While oven preheats:
 • Chop apple and walnuts.
 • Combine apple mixture,
   and top rolls.

2. Bake cakes.

3. Drizzle with icing.

Individual Apple-Walnut Coffee Cakes

prep: 12 minutes • **cook:** 24 minutes   *PointsPlus* value per serving: 6

These individual cakes are a cross between apple-walnut-streusel coffee cake and iced cinnamon rolls, all in one muffin.

 1 cup finely chopped unpeeled Braeburn apple (1 medium)
 ⅓ cup chopped walnuts
 3 tablespoons brown sugar, divided
 1 tablespoon light stick butter, melted
 1 (12.4-ounce) can reduced-fat cinnamon rolls
Cooking spray

1. Preheat oven to 375°.

2. Combine apple, walnuts, 2 tablespoons brown sugar, and butter in a small bowl.

3. Separate cinnamon rolls, reserving icing. Place 1 roll in each of 8 muffin cups coated with cooking spray. Spoon apple mixture over cinnamon rolls; sprinkle with 1 tablespoon brown sugar.

4. Bake at 375° for 24 minutes or until lightly browned and puffed. Remove from muffin cups, and place on a wire rack.

5. While cakes bake, place reserved icing in a microwave-safe bowl. Microwave at HIGH 20 seconds or until pourable. Drizzle warm icing over cakes. Serve immediately. **Yield:** 8 servings (serving size: 1 cake).

Per serving: CALORIES 209; FAT 7.4g (sat 1.7g, mono 2.5g, poly 2.8g); PROTEIN 2.8g; CARB 33g; FIBER 1.4g; CHOL 2mg; IRON 0.9mg; SODIUM 353mg; CALC 10mg

Mediterranean Goat Cheese
Spread | page 10

33

Tomato-Basil Bruschetta | page 11

34

Frozen Blueberry-Lime Margaritas
| page 22

Sunny-Side-Up Vegetable Skillet | page 49

Eggs Benedict | page 50

Ham, Bell Pepper, and Cheddar Omelet for Two | page 52

Rustic Spinach, Bacon, and Egg Breakfast Pizza | page 52

Breakfast Burritos | page 56

**Lemon-Blueberry Breakfast
Parfaits** | page 60

Southwestern Chicken and White Bean Soup | page 70

Chicken Pasta Soup | page 69

Mushroom and Swiss Paninis | page 73

Easy Pulled Pork Sandwiches | page 77

Arugula, Pear, and Gorgonzola Salad | page 87

Caesar Romaine with
Black Bread Croutons | page 85

47

Spicy Vegetable Salad with Pasta | page 86

pictured on page 36

Sunny-Side-Up Vegetable Skillet

prep: 12 minutes • **cook:** 23 minutes   *PointsPlus* value per serving: 5

This one-dish recipe's hearty medley of vegetables is a great way to simplify breakfast.

Cooking spray
2 medium potatoes, microwave-cooked, peeled, cooled, and diced
1¼ cups sliced mushrooms
¾ cup vertically sliced onion
¾ cup sliced red bell pepper
4 pasteurized large eggs
½ teaspoon salt
½ teaspoon freshly ground black pepper
2 tablespoons minced fresh chives (optional)

1. Preheat oven to 375°.
2. Heat a medium-sized nonstick ovenproof skillet over medium-high heat. Coat pan with cooking spray. Add potato to pan; coat potato with cooking spray. Cover and cook 7 minutes or until lightly browned, stirring occasionally. Transfer to a plate, and keep warm.
3. Coat pan with cooking spray. Add mushrooms, onion, and bell pepper; cook 6 minutes or until tender, stirring occasionally. Gently stir in potato. Crack eggs, 1 at a time, into potato mixture; sprinkle eggs with salt and black pepper.
4. Bake, uncovered, at 375° for 10 minutes.
5. Divide vegetable mixture and eggs among 4 plates. Sprinkle eggs with chives, if desired. Serve immediately. **Yield:** 4 servings (serving size: 1 egg and about 1 cup potato mixture).

Per serving: CALORIES 185; FAT 5.2g (sat 1.6g, mono 1.9g, poly 0.7g); PROTEIN 9.8g; CARB 25.7g; FIBER 2.5g; CHOL 212mg; IRON 2.2mg; SODIUM 375mg; CALC 50mg

Menu
PointsPlus value
per serving: 7

**Sunny-Side-Up
Vegetable Skillet**

**1 slice high-fiber
whole-wheat toast**
PointsPlus value
per serving: 2

Game Plan

1. While potatoes microwave:
• Slice vegetables.
• Preheat oven, and heat skillet.

2. While egg mixture bakes:
• Toast bread.

pictured on page 37

Eggs Benedict

prep: 2 minutes • **cook:** 13 minutes   *PointsPlus* value per serving: 5

Menu
PointsPlus value per serving: 6

Eggs Benedict

1 cup light orange juice
PointsPlus value per serving: 1

Game Plan

1. While eggs poach:
  • Cook Hollandaise sauce.

2. Microwave bacon, and toast muffin halves.

3. Assemble muffins, bacon, eggs, and sauce on plates.

For food-safety reasons, we cooked the eggs in this recipe until the yolks were firm. If you don't like your eggs set, use pasteurized eggs, and cook to desired degree of doneness.

    4 large eggs
    Cooking spray
    ½ cup fat-free milk
    1 (0.9-ounce) package Hollandaise sauce mix
    1 tablespoon light stick butter
    4 slices Canadian bacon
    2 (2-ounce) light multigrain English muffins, split and toasted
    ½ teaspoon freshly ground black pepper
    Fresh chives, cut into 1½-inch pieces (optional)

1. Add water to a medium-sized skillet, filling two-thirds full; bring to a boil. Reduce heat; simmer. Break 1 egg into each of 4 (6-ounce) custard cups coated with cooking spray. Place custard cups in simmering water in pan. Cover pan; cook 8 minutes. Remove custard cups from water.

2. While eggs cook, place milk and 4½ teaspoons sauce mix in a small saucepan, reserving remaining sauce mix for another use; stir with a whisk until blended. Add butter to milk mixture. Cook, stirring constantly, over medium heat until sauce thickens.

3. Place bacon slices on a paper plate; cover slices with a paper towel. Microwave at HIGH 10 seconds or just until warm. Place 1 muffin half on each of 4 plates. Place 1 bacon slice on each muffin half. Run a small spatula around outside edge of each egg. Release eggs from custard cups, and invert onto bacon slices. Top each egg with 2 tablespoons sauce; sprinkle sauce with pepper. Garnish with chives, if desired. Serve immediately. **Yield:** 4 servings (serving size: 1 plate).

Per serving: CALORIES 193; FAT 8.4g (sat 3g, mono 3g, poly 1g); PROTEIN 14.6g; CARB 18.4g; FIBER 4.1g; CHOL 230mg; IRON 1.7mg; SODIUM 619mg; CALC 107mg

Asparagus-Mushroom Omelet

prep: 11 minutes • **cook:** 11 minutes *PointsPlus* value per serving: 6

This hearty veggie-cheese omelet is perfect for brunch or whenever you're craving breakfast for dinner.

- 1 teaspoon olive oil, divided
- Cooking spray
- 1 cup sliced mushrooms
- ½ cup chopped asparagus (about 6 spears)
- 2 tablespoons chopped green onions
- 4 large eggs
- 1 large egg white
- 2 teaspoons chopped fresh parsley
- ¼ teaspoon salt
- ⅛ teaspoon freshly ground black pepper
- 2 ounces reduced-fat shredded Swiss cheese (about ½ cup)

1. Heat ½ teaspoon oil in a medium-sized nonstick skillet coated with cooking spray over medium-high heat. Add mushrooms, asparagus, and green onions; sauté 5 minutes or until crisp-tender. Remove from pan, set aside, and keep warm.

2. Combine eggs, egg white, and next 3 ingredients in a bowl, stirring well with a whisk. Heat ½ teaspoon oil in pan. Add egg mixture to pan; cook until edges begin to set (about 2 minutes). Gently lift edges of omelet with a spatula, and tilt pan so uncooked portion flows underneath. Continue cooking until center is just set (about 4 minutes).

3. Spoon vegetable mixture over half of omelet, and sprinkle cheese over vegetable mixture. Loosen omelet with spatula, and fold in half. Cut omelet in half crosswise, and serve immediately. **Yield:** 2 servings (serving size: ½ omelet).

Per serving: CALORIES 241; FAT 13.9g (sat 4.4g, mono 5.9g, poly 1.8g); PROTEIN 24.1g; CARB 4.9g; FIBER 1.3g; CHOL 432mg; IRON 3mg; SODIUM 533mg; CALC 330mg

Menu

PointsPlus value
per serving: 6

Asparagus-Mushroom Omelet

1 grapefruit half
PointsPlus value
per serving: 0

Game Plan

1. Chop vegetables.

2. While skillet heats:
- Whisk egg mixture.
- Cut grapefruit.

3. Cook omelet, and serve immediately.

pictured on page 38

Ham, Bell Pepper, and Cheddar Omelet for Two

Menu
PointsPlus value
per serving: 6

Ham, Bell Pepper,
and Cheddar Omelet for Two

1 cup light orange juice
PointsPlus value
per serving: 1

Game Plan

1. While skillet heats:
   • Measure ingredients.

2. Sauté bell pepper and ham.

3. Cook omelet, and serve
   immediately.

prep: 1 minute • **cook:** 13 minutes   *PointsPlus* value per serving: 5

Butter-flavored cooking spray
⅔ cup refrigerated prechopped tricolor bell pepper
½ cup prechopped ham
1 cup egg substitute
2 ounces reduced-fat shredded sharp cheddar cheese (about ½ cup)
⅛ teaspoon freshly ground black pepper

1. Heat a 10-inch nonstick skillet over medium heat. Coat pan with cooking spray. Add bell pepper and ham; sauté 3 to 4 minutes. Remove from pan; set aside, and keep warm.
2. Wipe pan with a paper towel; recoat pan with cooking spray. Pour egg substitute into pan; sprinkle with cheese. Cover, reduce heat, and cook 8 minutes or until set (do not stir). Spoon bell pepper mixture over omelet; fold omelet in half. Cut omelet in half crosswise, and sprinkle with black pepper; serve immediately. **Yield:** 2 servings (serving size: ½ omelet).

Per serving: CALORIES 178; FAT 6.6g (sat 3.5g, mono 1.8g, poly 0.2g); PROTEIN 24.5g; CARB 6.8g; FIBER 0.9g; CHOL 33mg; IRON 3.6mg; SODIUM 703mg; CALC 493mg

pictured on page 39

Rustic Spinach, Bacon, and Egg Breakfast Pizza

Menu
PointsPlus value
per serving: 6

Rustic Spinach, Bacon,
and Egg Breakfast Pizza

1 cup pineapple cubes
PointsPlus value
per serving: 0

Game Plan

1. While oven preheats:
   • Thaw spinach in
     microwave.
   • Cook bacon.

2. Bake dough.

3. Assemble pizza.

4. While pizza bakes:
   • Cut pineapple.

prep: 5 minutes • **cook:** 23 minutes   *PointsPlus* value per serving: 6

1 (11-ounce) can refrigerated thin pizza crust dough
Cooking spray
1 (10-ounce) package frozen creamed spinach, thawed
8 pasteurized large eggs
3 tablespoons grated fresh Parmesan cheese
4 lower-sodium bacon slices, cooked

1. Preheat oven to 400°.
2. Unroll dough; press into bottom and ¼ inch up sides of a 15 x 10–inch jelly-roll pan coated with cooking spray. Bake at 400° for 5 minutes or until set.
3. Spread creamed spinach over crust. Carefully crack eggs, evenly spaced for 8 servings, on top of pizza. Sprinkle with cheese.
4. Bake at 400° for 18 minutes or until crust is brown and eggs are soft-set. Remove from oven; crumble bacon over pizza. Serve immediately. **Yield:** 8 servings (serving size: ⅛ pizza).

Per serving: CALORIES 236; FAT 11.2g (sat 3.5g, mono 3.5g, poly 2.8g); PROTEIN 12.5g; CARB 21.5g; FIBER 1g; CHOL 216mg; IRON 1.9mg; SODIUM 555mg; CALC 97mg

Fresh Herbed Omelet with Goat Cheese

prep: 5 minutes • **cook:** 8 minutes   *PointsPlus* value per serving: 5

Tangy goat cheese pairs well with the earthy flavors of fresh basil, oregano, and thyme. Enjoy this savory omelet for breakfast with fresh fruit.

  1   tablespoon chopped fresh basil
  2   tablespoons fat-free milk
  2   teaspoons chopped fresh oregano
  2   teaspoons chopped fresh thyme
  ¼   teaspoon salt
  ⅛   teaspoon freshly ground black pepper
  2   large eggs
  2   large egg whites
  1   teaspoon butter
  1   ounce crumbled goat cheese (about ¼ cup)

1. Combine first 8 ingredients in a bowl, stirring with a whisk.

2. Melt butter in a 9-inch nonstick skillet over medium heat. Pour egg mixture into pan. As mixture starts to cook, gently lift edges of omelet with a spatula, and tilt pan so uncooked portion flows underneath. Cook just until set (about 5 minutes).

3. Sprinkle cheese over omelet. Fold omelet in half; cover and reduce heat to low. Cook 2 minutes. Cut omelet in half crosswise. Serve immediately. **Yield:** 2 servings (serving size: ½ omelet).

Per serving: CALORIES 190; FAT 13.1g (sat 7g, mono 4.3g, poly 1.3g); PROTEIN 15g; CARB 2.4g; FIBER 0.2g; CHOL 233mg; IRON 1.5mg; SODIUM 542mg; CALC 122mg

Menu
PointsPlus value
per serving: 5

Fresh Herbed Omelet with Goat Cheese

1 cup strawberry slices
PointsPlus value
per serving: 0

Game Plan

1. While skillet heats:
  • Chop herbs.
  • Combine egg mixture.
  • Slice strawberries.

2. Cook omelet, and serve immediately.

Menu

PointsPlus value
per serving: 6

Cheesy Hash Brown–
Sausage Pie

1 large cantaloupe slice
PointsPlus value
per serving: 0

Game Plan

1. Thaw hash browns.

2. While oven preheats:
- Brown sausage.
- Combine milk and egg substitute.

3. While pie bakes:
- Slice cantaloupe.

Cheesy Hash Brown–Sausage Pie

prep: 7 minutes • **cook:** 28 minutes   *PointsPlus* value per serving: 6

Sausage and hash browns combine in this cheesy dish that puts other breakfast casseroles to shame.

- ¾ cup sliced green onions (about 1 bunch)
- 2 garlic cloves, minced
- 1 (12-ounce) package 50%-less-fat ground pork sausage
- ¾ teaspoon salt
- ½ teaspoon freshly ground black pepper
- 1 (30-ounce) package frozen country-style hash brown potatoes, thawed
- 1½ cups fat-free milk
- 1 cup egg substitute
- 6 ounces reduced-fat shredded sharp cheddar cheese (about 1½ cups)
- 1 medium tomato, thinly sliced

1. Preheat oven to 450°.

2. Place first 3 ingredients in a 12-inch ovenproof skillet, and cook over medium-high heat 7 minutes or until sausage is browned, stirring to crumble sausage. Stir in salt, pepper, and hash browns; cook over medium-high heat 3 minutes.

3. Combine milk and egg substitute, stirring with a whisk. Stir in 1 cup cheese; pour over hash brown mixture. Sprinkle with ½ cup cheese.

4. Bake at 450° for 18 minutes or until set and top begins to brown. Top with sliced tomato. **Yield:** 10 servings (serving size: 1 wedge).

Per serving: CALORIES 245; FAT 9.9g (sat 4.6g, mono 0.9g, poly 0.1g); PROTEIN 16g; CARB 20.8g; FIBER 1.6g; CHOL 37mg; IRON 1mg; SODIUM 620mg; CALC 183mg

Sausage and Spinach Frittata

prep: 3 minutes • **cook:** 14 minutes   *PointsPlus* value per serving: 5

This quick omelet combines sweet onion, tender chicken sausage, and spinach for a delicious, low-calorie start to the day. For an extra kick, stir ¼ teaspoon crushed red pepper or a few dashes of hot sauce into the egg mixture. Serve leftovers chilled for lunch paired with a mesclun greens salad (2 cups of greens without dressing has a *PointsPlus* value of 0).

  Cooking spray
 1   cup thinly vertically sliced sweet onion
 ¼   teaspoon freshly ground black pepper
 1   (6-ounce) package fresh baby spinach
 2   links precooked Italian chicken sausage, sliced
 8   large eggs
 1.3 ounces preshredded reduced-fat 4-cheese Mexican blend cheese
       (about ⅓ cup)

1. Preheat broiler.

2. Heat a 10-inch ovenproof skillet over medium heat. Coat pan with cooking spray. Add onion to pan; coat onion with cooking spray, and cook 5 minutes, stirring occasionally. Add pepper and spinach; cook 1 minute or just until spinach wilts. Remove spinach mixture from pan; keep warm.

3. Coat pan with cooking spray. Add sausage; cook 2 minutes or until thoroughly heated. Return spinach mixture to pan.

4. Crack 4 eggs into a bowl. Separate 4 eggs, adding egg whites to eggs in bowl and reserving yolks for another use. Stir egg mixture with a whisk until foamy. Pour egg mixture into pan, and cook over medium heat. Do not stir until a layer of egg has set on bottom of pan. Gently lift edges of omelet with a rubber spatula, and tilt pan to allow any uncooked egg mixture to flow underneath. Continue to cook until top is almost set.

5. Sprinkle top of frittata with cheese. Broil 1 minute or until top is golden brown. Cut frittata into 6 wedges. Serve immediately. **Yield:** 6 servings (serving size: 1 wedge).

Per serving: CALORIES 191; FAT 11.8g (sat 4g, mono 2.8g, poly 1.3g); PROTEIN 15.6g; CARB 6.1g; FIBER 2g; CHOL 275mg; IRON 2.1mg; SODIUM 408mg; CALC 118mg

Menu
PointsPlus value
per serving: 8

Sausage and Spinach Frittata

1 (6-ounce) carton strawberry fat-free Greek yogurt
PointsPlus value
per serving: 3

Game Plan

1. While skillet heats:
   • Slice onion and sausage.
   • Combine eggs and egg whites.

2. Sauté vegetables and sausage separately.

3. Cook egg mixture.

pictured on page 40

Breakfast Burritos

prep: 4 minutes • **cook:** 11 minutes   *PointsPlus* value per serving: 8

This burrito can be a great on-the-go breakfast—just wrap it in foil. Serve each burrito with a tablespoon of salsa on the side, if you like. The *PointsPlus* value will be the same.

½ cup refrigerated diced potatoes with onion
1 tablespoon water
¼ pound mild turkey Italian sausage
5 large eggs
Cooking spray
4 (8-inch) 96% fat-free whole-wheat tortillas
2 ounces reduced-fat shredded white cheddar cheese with jalapeño peppers (about ½ cup)
½ peeled avocado, sliced
2 tablespoons chopped fresh cilantro (optional)
¼ cup fresh salsa (optional)

1. Place potatoes and 1 tablespoon water in a microwave-safe bowl. Cover bowl with heavy-duty plastic wrap; vent. Microwave at HIGH 4 minutes.

2. Cook sausage and potatoes in a large nonstick skillet over medium heat 6 minutes or until sausage is browned, stirring to crumble. Remove from pan, and keep warm.

3. Separate 4 eggs, placing whites in a bowl; reserve yolks for another use. Combine egg whites and remaining egg in bowl, stirring with a whisk. Heat a medium-sized nonstick skillet over medium-low heat; coat pan with cooking spray. Add beaten eggs to pan. Cook, without stirring, until mixture sets on bottom. Draw a spatula across bottom of pan to form curds. Continue until egg mixture is thick, but still moist; do not stir constantly. Remove from pan immediately.

4. Warm tortillas according to package directions. Top tortillas with egg, sausage mixture, cheese, avocado, and, if desired, cilantro; roll up. Serve with salsa, if desired. **Yield:** 4 servings (serving size: 1 burrito).

Per serving: CALORIES 290; FAT 11.2g (sat 2.8g, mono 4.9g, poly 1.8g); PROTEIN 18.6g; CARB 31.2g; FIBER 4.5g; CHOL 77mg; IRON 2.4mg; SODIUM 749mg; CALC 139mg

"Sausage" Breakfast Strata

prep: 21 minutes • **cook:** 60 minutes • **other:** 8 hours and 40 minutes

PointsPlus value per serving: 7

Make this cheesy vegetarian casserole a day ahead so the only work that will need to be done before breakfast is sticking it in the oven to bake. Weekend houseguests won't have a clue they're getting a healthy dose of soy protein with every delicious bite.

1 (8-ounce) package frozen veggie breakfast sausage links
Cooking spray
1 tablespoon light stick butter
1 (8-ounce) package presliced mushrooms
⅔ cup chopped green onions (about 6 onions)
⅔ cup chopped tomato
½ teaspoon salt, divided
8 slices light white bread, cubed
1 (8-ounce) block reduced-fat sharp cheddar cheese, shredded
2 cups 1% low-fat milk
½ cup egg substitute
1 teaspoon dry mustard
3 large eggs

1. Place frozen sausage in a large skillet coated with cooking spray; cook over medium heat until thawed and lightly browned on all sides, stirring frequently (about 8 minutes). Remove from pan to cool. Cut sausage into ½-inch-thick slices.
2. Heat butter in pan over medium heat. Add mushrooms, and sauté 4 minutes. Add onions; sauté 2 minutes. Remove from heat; stir in tomato and ¼ teaspoon salt.
3. Coat an 11 x 7–inch glass or ceramic baking dish with cooking spray, and place half of bread cubes in bottom of dish. Top with half of sausage, half of vegetable mixture, and half of cheese. Repeat layers with remaining bread cubes, sausage, vegetable mixture, and cheese.
4. Combine milk, egg substitute, mustard, eggs, and ¼ teaspoon salt in a bowl, stirring with a whisk. Pour mixture over casserole. Cover and refrigerate at least 8 hours.
5. Let casserole stand at room temperature 30 minutes before baking.
6. Preheat oven to 350°.
7. Bake at 350° for 45 to 50 minutes or until center is set. Let stand 10 minutes.
Yield: 8 servings (serving size: ⅛ strata).

Per serving: CALORIES 262; FAT 12g (sat 5.8g, mono 2.6g, poly 1.6g); PROTEIN 22.2g; CARB 17.1g; FIBER 4.6g; CHOL 104mg; IRON 3.1mg; SODIUM 761mg; CALC 333mg

---

Menu
PointsPlus value
per serving: 7

"Sausage" Breakfast Strata

1 orange, cut into wedges
PointsPlus value
per serving: 0

Game Plan

1. While sausage browns:
• Chop onions and tomato.
• Cube bread.
• Shred cheese.

2. Assemble strata, and let stand.

3. While strata bakes:
• Slice oranges.

Menu

PointsPlus value
per serving: 10

Easy Huevos Rancheros

**Cantaloupe
with Honey and Lime**
PointsPlus value
per serving: 1

Game Plan

1. Chop cilantro, and drain
tomatoes.

2. Rinse, drain, and mash
beans.

3. Cook eggs, and assemble
burritos.

4. Cut cantaloupe, and drizzle
with honey and lime.

Easy Huevos Rancheros

prep: 8 minutes • **cook:** 6 minutes   *PointsPlus* value per serving: 9

  2 tablespoons chopped fresh cilantro
  2 teaspoons fresh lime juice
  1 (10-ounce) can diced tomatoes and green chiles, drained
  1 (15-ounce) can black beans, rinsed and drained
  1 tablespoon butter
  4 large eggs
  4 (8-inch) flour tortillas
  2 ounces preshredded reduced-fat 4-cheese Mexican blend cheese (about ½ cup)

1. Combine cilantro, lime juice, and tomatoes in a small bowl; set aside.
2. Place black beans in a small microwave-safe dish; partially mash beans with
a fork. Cover and microwave at HIGH 2 minutes.
3. Melt butter in a large nonstick skillet. Add eggs; cook over medium-high
heat 1 to 2 minutes on each side or until done (do not break yolks).
4. Warm tortillas according to package directions. Spread beans over tortillas; top
each with 1 egg. Top with tomato mixture and cheese. **Yield:** 4 servings (serving
size: 1 tortilla, ⅛ cup beans, 1 egg, ¼ cup tomato mixture, and 2 tablespoons cheese).

Per serving: CALORIES 351; FAT 13.7g (sat 5.9g, mono 4.1g, poly 1.3g); PROTEIN 19g; CARB 37.1g; FIBER 4.2g; CHOL 224mg; IRON 3.7mg; SODIUM 709mg; CALC 254mg

Cantaloupe with Honey and Lime

prep: 5 minutes   *PointsPlus* value per serving: 1

**Honey and lime juice add a burst of flavor to plain cantaloupe which
guarantees to brighten your breakfast any morning.**

  ½ cantaloupe
  4 teaspoons honey
  4 teaspoons fresh lime juice

1. Cut cantaloupe into 4 wedges. Cut slits into each wedge, cutting into but not
through rind. Drizzle each wedge with 1 teaspoon honey and 1 teaspoon lime
juice. Serve immediately. **Yield:** 4 servings (serving size: 1 wedge).

Per serving: CALORIES 46; FAT 0.1g (sat 0g, mono 0g, poly 0.1g); PROTEIN 0.6g; CARB 11.8g; FIBER 0.6g; CHOL 0mg; IRON 0.2mg; SODIUM 11mg; CALC 7mg

Meatless Hash and Eggs

prep: 3 minutes • **cook:** 16 minutes   *PointsPlus* value per serving: 7

This meat-free dish, adapted from a traditional recipe for corned beef and hash, earned one of our Test Kitchen's highest ratings.

2½   cups frozen shredded hash brown potatoes
1½   cups frozen meatless crumbles
1½   cups prechopped tomato, green bell pepper, and onion mix
½   teaspoon salt
¼   teaspoon freshly ground black pepper
1   tablespoon olive oil
Cooking spray
4   large eggs

1. Combine first 5 ingredients in a medium bowl.
2. Heat oil in a large nonstick skillet coated with cooking spray over medium heat. Add potato mixture, and cook 5 to 7 minutes or until potato mixture is thoroughly heated, stirring occasionally. Form 4 (3-inch) indentations in potato mixture using the back of a spoon. Break 1 egg into each indentation. Cover and cook 10 minutes or until eggs are done. **Yield:** 4 servings (serving size: 1 egg and 1 cup potato mixture).

Per serving: CALORIES 271; FAT 10.8g (sat 2.3g, mono 4.7g, poly 3g); PROTEIN 15.2g; CARB 30.3g; FIBER 3.9g; CHOL 212mg; IRON 3.4mg; SODIUM 527mg; CALC 59mg

Menu
PointsPlus value per serving: 7

Meatless Hash and Eggs

1 cup unsweetened applesauce
PointsPlus value per serving: 0

Game Plan

1. While skillet heats:
   • Measure ingredients.

2. Cook potato mixture, and add eggs.

3. Portion applesauce.

Berry-Banana Smoothie

prep: 5 minutes   *PointsPlus* value per serving: 4

1½   cups frozen mixed berries, thawed and drained
2   (6-ounce) cartons organic smooth and creamy French vanilla low-fat yogurt
½   (16-ounce) package silken tofu, drained
2   cups ripe banana slices, frozen (about 2 bananas)
2   cups ice cubes
Fresh blueberries, raspberries, or strawberries (optional)

1. Place 1½ cups mixed berries in a blender or food processor; process 20 seconds or until smooth. Pour berry mixture through a sieve into a bowl, pressing with the back of a spoon to remove as much juice as possible. Discard pulp and seeds.
2. Place berry juice, yogurt, and tofu in blender; process until smooth. Add banana slices and ice; process until smooth. Pour mixture into 5 glasses; garnish with berries, if desired. Serve immediately. **Yield:** 5 servings (serving size: 1 cup).

Per serving: CALORIES 137; FAT 1.7g (sat 0.4g, mono 0.4g, poly 0.5g); PROTEIN 5.5g; CARB 26g; FIBER 2.8g; CHOL 2mg; IRON 0.6mg; SODIUM 42mg; CALC 136mg

Menu
PointsPlus value per serving: 8

Berry-Banana Smoothie

1 toasted whole-wheat English muffin half with 2 teaspoons peanut butter
PointsPlus value per serving: 4

Game Plan

1. Drain thawed berries and tofu.

2. Slice banana.

3. Toast muffin halves.

4. Process smoothie.

pictured on page 41

Lemon-Blueberry Breakfast Parfaits

prep: 5 minutes   *PointsPlus* value per serving: 8

Assemble these parfaits in decorative glasses for an impressive presentation—or in a disposable cup for an easy on-the-go breakfast.

    1   tablespoon grated fresh lemon rind
    3   (6-ounce) cartons blueberry fat-free Greek yogurt
    2   cups blueberries
    1   cup low-fat granola
    ¼   cup chopped walnuts, toasted

1. Combine lemon rind and yogurt. Layer ¼ cup yogurt mixture, ¼ cup blueberries, and ¼ cup granola in each of 4 parfait glasses. Repeat layers using 3 tablespoons yogurt mixture and ¼ cup blueberries for each parfait. Top each serving with 1 tablespoon walnuts. **Yield:** 4 servings (serving size: 1 parfait).

Per serving: CALORIES 291; FAT 6.3g (sat 0.8g, mono 1.2g, poly 4g); PROTEIN 14.1g; CARB 46.9g; FIBER 3.9g; CHOL 0mg; IRON 1.3mg; SODIUM 103mg; CALC 173mg

Sausage Patties

prep: 5 minutes • **cook:** 8 minutes per batch   *PointsPlus* value per serving: 4

While these are best when served immediately after cooking, you can refrigerate the uncooked mixture in a sealed container for one day.

    2   teaspoons dried rubbed sage
    1   teaspoon pepper
    ¾   teaspoon garlic powder
    ½   teaspoon salt
    ½   teaspoon onion powder
    1   pound lean ground pork
    1   pound ground turkey breast
    Cooking spray

1. Combine first 7 ingredients in a large bowl. Shape mixture into 16 (½-inch-thick) patties.
2. Heat a large nonstick skillet over medium heat. Coat pan with cooking spray. Add half of patties; cook 4 minutes on each side or until browned and done. Remove patties from pan; keep warm. Repeat procedure with remaining patties. **Yield:** 8 servings (serving size: 2 patties).

Per serving: CALORIES 159; FAT 6.7g (sat 2.5g, mono 3g, poly 0.9g); PROTEIN 24.8g; CARB 0.6g; FIBER 0.2g; CHOL 56mg; IRON 1.3mg; SODIUM 213mg; CALC 9mg

Soups & Sandwiches

Honey-Gingered Carrot Soup

Menu
PointsPlus value
per serving: 5

Honey-Gingered Carrot Soup

Three-Seed Breadsticks
(page 155)
PointsPlus value
per serving: 2

Game Plan

1. While soup ingredients cook:
   - Preheat oven for breadsticks.
   - Combine cereal and seed mixture.

2. Bake breadsticks.

3. Process soup.

prep: 3 minutes • **cook:** 12 minutes • **other:** 1 minute

PointsPlus value per serving: 3

Honey, orange, and ginger pair beautifully with carrots. In this soup, pureeing the ingredients helps bring out and marry all of the flavors: You'll get sweetness, tang, and spice in every spoonful.

- 3 cups fat-free, lower-sodium chicken broth
- ½ cup frozen chopped onion
- 1 tablespoon minced peeled fresh ginger
- 1 teaspoon grated fresh orange rind
- ¼ teaspoon freshly ground black pepper
- 2 (10-ounce) packages frozen sliced honey-glazed carrots, thawed
- ¼ cup plain fat-free yogurt (optional)
- Thyme sprigs (optional)

1. Combine first 6 ingredients in a large saucepan; bring to a boil. Reduce heat; simmer 2 minutes or until carrot is tender.

2. Place half of soup mixture in a blender or food processor. Remove center piece of blender lid (to allow steam to escape); secure blender lid on blender. Place a clean towel over opening in blender lid (to avoid splatters). Blend 30 seconds or until smooth. Pour pureed mixture into a large bowl. Repeat procedure with remaining soup mixture. Ladle soup into 4 bowls; garnish with 1 tablespoon yogurt and thyme sprigs, if desired. **Yield:** 4 servings (serving size: 1¼ cups).

Per serving: CALORIES 160; FAT 4g (sat 0.6g, mono 0g, poly 0g); PROTEIN 3.7g; CARB 20.7g; FIBER 3.8g; CHOL 0mg; IRON 0.1mg; SODIUM 664mg; CALC 26mg

Menu
PointsPlus value
per serving: 6

Tomato and Basil Soup

Parmesan-Basil Biscuits
(page 159)
PointsPlus value
per serving: 3

Game Plan

1. Chop tomatoes and basil.

2. While biscuits bake:
   - Combine and heat soup ingredients.

3. Stir basil and olive oil into soup.

Tomato and Basil Soup

prep: 1 minute • **cook:** 7 minutes • **other:** 3 minutes   *PointsPlus* value per serving: 3

- 1 (14½-ounce) can Italian-style stewed tomatoes, undrained
- 1 teaspoon sugar
- 1 (14-ounce) can fat-free, lower-sodium chicken broth
- 2 tablespoons chopped fresh basil
- 1 tablespoon extra-virgin olive oil

1. Place tomatoes in a medium saucepan. Using kitchen shears, snip tomatoes until coarsely chopped. Stir in sugar and broth. Bring to a boil; cover, reduce heat, and simmer 5 minutes. Remove from heat; stir in basil and oil. Let soup stand 3 minutes. Ladle soup into bowls. **Yield:** 3 servings (serving size: 1 cup).

Per serving: CALORIES 95; FAT 5g (sat 0.7g, mono 3.7g, poly 0.3g); PROTEIN 3.2g; CARB 11.1g; FIBER 1.2g; CHOL 0mg; IRON 0.9mg; SODIUM 673mg; CALC 48mg

Roasted Garlic and Vidalia Onion Soup

prep: 14 minutes • **cook:** 1 hour and 35 minutes   *PointsPlus* value per serving: 4

For a nonalcoholic version, substitute chicken broth or water for the wine.

1   whole garlic head
Cooking spray
4   Vidalia or other sweet onions (about 2¾ pounds), peeled and cut into eighths
6   cups fat-free, lower-sodium chicken broth
⅓   cup dry white wine
1   teaspoon dried thyme
1   bay leaf
1   tablespoon butter
½   teaspoon salt
¼   teaspoon freshly ground black pepper
8   (½-inch-thick) slices diagonally cut French bread baguette
4   ounces shredded Swiss cheese (about 1 cup)

1. Preheat oven to 375°.
2. Cut off top of garlic head; discard. Spray garlic head generously with cooking spray; wrap in foil.
3. Arrange onion on a jelly-roll pan coated with cooking spray. Spray onion with cooking spray. Place garlic on pan; bake at 375° for 1 hour or until onion is tender and browned, stirring onion after 40 minutes.
4. Unwrap garlic. Squeeze to extract garlic pulp; discard white papery skin. Combine garlic pulp and onion in a Dutch oven. Add broth and next 3 ingredients; bring to a boil. Cover, reduce heat, and simmer 30 minutes. Stir in butter, salt, and pepper. Discard bay leaf.
5. While onion mixture simmers, place baguette slices on a baking sheet coated with cooking spray. Top each slice with 2 tablespoons cheese. Bake at 375° for 5 minutes or until cheese melts. Serve with soup. **Yield:** 8 servings (serving size: about 1 cup soup and 1 baguette slice).

Per serving: CALORIES 159; FAT 5.3g (sat 3.3g, mono 1.4g, poly 0.2g); PROTEIN 8.6g; CARB 20.9g; FIBER 1.8g; CHOL 16mg; IRON 1.1mg; SODIUM 690mg; CALC 178mg

Menu
PointsPlus value per serving: 5

Roasted Garlic and Vidalia Onion Soup

1 cup mixed salad greens with 2 tablespoons light balsamic vinaigrette dressing
PointsPlus value per serving: 1

Game Plan

1. Roast garlic and onions.

2. While soup ingredients simmer:
• Slice baguette, and shred cheese.
• Tear salad greens.

3. Cook bread slices.

4. Toss salad with dressing.

Menu

PointsPlus value
per serving: 6

Leek and Potato Soup

1 cup mixed fruit salad
PointsPlus value
per serving: 0

Game Plan

1. Chop vegetables.

2. While soup simmers:
• Cut fruit.
• Mince chives.

3. Process soup.

4. Top soup with sour cream and chives.

Leek and Potato Soup

prep: 18 minutes • **cook:** 42 minutes • **other:** 3 minutes

PointsPlus value per serving: 6

Serve this soup warm on a winter day or chilled on a summer evening.

- 1 tablespoon olive oil
- 3 cups chopped leek (white and pale green parts only; about 2 leeks)
- 2 tablespoons all-purpose flour
- 6 cups fat-free, lower-sodium chicken broth
- ¼ teaspoon freshly ground black pepper
- 6 small red potatoes, peeled and cut into ¾-inch pieces (about 3 cups)
- 1⅓ cups light sour cream, divided
- 3 teaspoons fresh lemon juice
- 2 tablespoons minced fresh chives

1. Heat oil in a Dutch oven over medium-high heat. Add leek; cook, covered, 5 minutes or until tender, stirring occasionally. Stir in flour; cook 2 minutes, stirring constantly. Add broth, pepper, and potato. Bring to a boil; cover, reduce heat, and simmer 30 minutes or until potato is very tender, stirring occasionally.
2. Place one-third of leek mixture in a blender. Remove center piece of blender lid (to allow steam to escape); secure blender lid on blender. Place a clean towel over opening in blender lid (to avoid splatters). Blend until smooth. Pour pureed mixture into pan. Repeat procedure twice with remaining leek mixture. Stir in 1 cup sour cream; cook 2 minutes over medium heat or until thoroughly heated. Stir in lemon juice. Ladle soup into bowls, and top with remaining ⅓ cup sour cream and chives.
Yield: 6 servings (serving size: 1⅓ cups soup, about 1 tablespoon sour cream, and 1 teaspoon chives).

Per serving: CALORIES 204; FAT 9g (sat 4.4g, mono 3.5g, poly 0.7g); PROTEIN 7.1g; CARB 25.4g; FIBER 2.1g; CHOL 21mg; IRON 1.7mg; SODIUM 605mg; CALC 89mg

Roasted Root Vegetable Soup

prep: 30 minutes • **cook:** 1 hour and 30 minutes

PointsPlus value per serving: 3

A dollop of sour cream stirred into each serving of soup blends all the other flavors together.

4	carrots, peeled
4	onions, peeled and halved
4	small red potatoes, halved
3	beets, peeled and halved
3	celery stalks, cut into 3-inch pieces
2	small sweet potatoes, peeled and quartered
	Cooking spray
6	cups organic vegetable broth
1	teaspoon dried thyme
½	teaspoon salt
¼	teaspoon freshly ground black pepper
10	tablespoons fat-free sour cream

1. Preheat oven to 425°.

2. Arrange first 6 ingredients in a single layer on a 17 x 12½–inch roasting pan coated with cooking spray; coat vegetables generously with cooking spray. Bake at 425° for 1 hour and 10 minutes or until tender and browned.

3. Chop vegetables into 1-inch pieces, and place in a Dutch oven over medium heat. Add ½ cup broth to roasting pan, scraping pan to loosen browned bits. Add browned bits, 5½ cups broth, thyme, salt, and pepper to vegetables. Bring to a boil; cover, reduce heat, and simmer 15 minutes. Ladle soup into bowls, and top with sour cream. **Yield:** 10 servings (serving size: 1 cup soup and 1 tablespoon sour cream).

Per serving: CALORIES 127; FAT 0.2g (sat 0.1g, mono 0g, poly 0.1g); PROTEIN 3.9g; CARB 27.4g; FIBER 3.9g; CHOL 3mg; IRON 1mg; SODIUM 538mg; CALC 68mg

Menu
PointsPlus value
per serving: 7

Roasted Root Vegetable Soup

1 ounce mozzarella cheese
PointsPlus value
per serving: 2

**1 slice high-fiber
whole-wheat toast**
PointsPlus value
per serving: 2

Game Plan

1. Cut vegetables.

2. Roast vegetables.

3. While soup simmers:
   • Melt cheese on toast.

Menu

PointsPlus value
per serving: 8

Warm Lentil Stew

½ cup deli coleslaw
PointsPlus value
per serving: 4

Game Plan

1. Chop and sauté onion.

2. Combine stew ingredients
   and boil.

3. Add spinach and remaining
   ingredients to stew.

4. Serve slaw with hot stew.

Warm Lentil Stew

prep: 2 minutes • **cook:** 38 minutes   *PointsPlus* value per serving: 4

    Olive oil–flavored cooking spray
  1 medium-sized red onion, chopped (about 2 cups)
  4 cups water
  ½ cup dried lentils
  ¾ teaspoon salt
  1 (14.5-ounce) can no-salt-added diced tomatoes, undrained
1½ tablespoons balsamic vinegar
  ½ teaspoon freshly ground black pepper
  1 (5- or 6-ounce) package fresh baby spinach

1. Heat a Dutch oven over medium heat. Coat pan with cooking spray. Add onion, and sauté 4 minutes.

2. Add 4 cups water and next 3 ingredients. Cover and bring to a boil; boil 30 minutes or until lentils are tender. Stir in vinegar, pepper, and spinach; cook 1 minute or until spinach wilts. Serve immediately. **Yield:** 4 servings (serving size: 1¼ cups).

Per serving: CALORIES 163; FAT 0.1g; PROTEIN 9.9g; CARB 33.8g; FIBER 8.3g; CHOL 0mg; IRON 4mg; SODIUM 549mg; CALC 66mg

Menu

PointsPlus value
per serving: 4

Sweet Pea Soup with Bacon

1 medium orange,
cut into wedges
PointsPlus value
per serving: 0

Game Plan

1. Cook bacon.

2. Sauté potatoes.

3. While soup simmers:
   • Crumble bacon.
   • Slice oranges.

4. Process soup in blender.

Sweet Pea Soup with Bacon

prep: 5 minutes • **cook:** 35 minutes   *PointsPlus* value per serving: 4

  6 slices lower-sodium bacon
1½ cups refrigerated diced potatoes with onions
  4 cups fat-free, lower-sodium chicken broth
  1 (16-ounce) package frozen petite green peas
  ½ cup fat-free half-and-half
  ¼ teaspoon freshly ground black pepper

1. Cook bacon in a large Dutch oven over medium-high heat 8 minutes or until crisp. Drain bacon on a paper towel; crumble. Reserve 2 tablespoons drippings in pan; discard excess drippings.

2. Add potatoes to drippings in pan, and sauté 5 minutes or until slightly brown. Add broth and peas to pan; bring to a boil. Cover, reduce heat to medium-low, and simmer 15 minutes. Place 4 cups soup in a blender. Remove center piece of blender lid (to allow steam to escape); secure blender lid on blender. Place a clean towel over opening in blender lid (to avoid splatters). Blend until smooth. Return pureed soup to pan; add half-and-half and pepper. Heat 4 minutes or until thoroughly heated. Ladle soup into bowls, and top with crumbled bacon. **Yield:** 6 servings (serving size: 1 cup soup and 1 tablespoon bacon).

Per serving: CALORIES 194; FAT 7.9g (sat 2.8g, mono 3.4g, poly 0.8g); PROTEIN 9.7g; CARB 20g; FIBER 4g; CHOL 13mg; IRON 1.4mg; SODIUM 637mg; CALC 31mg

Irish Beef Stew

prep: 23 minutes • **cook:** 8 hours and 30 minutes

PointsPlus value per serving: 8

Browning the lean beef tips before adding them to the slow cooker adds rich flavor to the stew. Cooking on LOW for a long time yields tender and juicy chunks of meat.

Cooking spray
1½   pounds beef tips, cut into 1-inch pieces
5   carrots, peeled and sliced into ½-inch-thick pieces (about 2 cups)
3   garlic cloves, minced
1   (20-ounce) bag refrigerated red potato wedges
1   medium onion, chopped
1½   cups plus 2 tablespoons water, divided
2   tablespoons tomato paste
1   teaspoon dried thyme
1   bay leaf
½   teaspoon freshly ground black pepper
2   (10½-ounce) cans beef consommé
2   tablespoons cornstarch

1. Heat a large nonstick skillet over medium-high heat; coat pan with cooking spray. Add beef, and cook 10 to 15 minutes or until thoroughly browned on all sides.

2. While beef cooks, place carrot and next 3 ingredients in a 4-quart electric slow cooker.

3. Place beef on top of vegetable mixture in cooker. Add 1½ cups water, tomato paste, and next 4 ingredients. Cover and cook on LOW 8 hours or until beef is tender. Discard bay leaf.

4. Combine 2 tablespoons water and cornstarch in a small bowl, stirring with a whisk until smooth; stir into beef mixture in cooker. Cover quickly, and increase heat to HIGH; cook 20 minutes or until gravy is thick. **Yield:** 6 servings (serving size: about 1½ cups).

Per serving: CALORIES 348; FAT 9g (sat 3.2g, mono 2.5g, poly 0.3g); PROTEIN 38g; CARB 26.1g; FIBER 4.5g; CHOL 98mg; IRON 3.9mg; SODIUM 689mg; CALC 44mg

Menu
PointsPlus value
per serving: 8

Irish Beef Stew

1 medium pear, cut into slices
PointsPlus value
per serving: 0

Game Plan

1. While beef browns:
• Chop onion, and mince garlic.
• Combine ingredients in slow cooker.

2. Cook stew for 8 hours.

3. Add and cook cornstarch mixture.

4. Slice pear.

Menu

PointsPlus value
per serving: 7

Mexican Chili

Jalapeño Corn Bread
Mini Muffins

Game Plan

1. Preheat oven.

2. Combine muffin batter.

3. While beef browns:
  • Bake muffins.
  • Chop onion, garlic, and chocolate.

4. Simmer chili.

Mexican Chili

prep: 3 minutes • **cook:** 15 minutes   *PointsPlus* value per serving: 4

Chocolate adds richness to the chili without making it sweet.

  1 pound ground round
  1 cup chopped onion (about 1 small onion)
  1 garlic clove, minced
  1 cup water
  2 tablespoons chili powder
  1 teaspoon ground cumin
  1 teaspoon salt
  ½ teaspoon dried oregano
  1 (14.5-ounce) can diced tomatoes, undrained
  1 ounce semisweet chocolate, coarsely chopped

1. Cook beef in a large saucepan over medium-high heat until browned, stirring to crumble. Drain, if necessary, and return beef to pan. Add onion and garlic to pan; cook 4 minutes or until tender. Add 1 cup water and remaining ingredients; cover and simmer 7 minutes. Serve immediately. **Yield:** 6 servings (serving size: ¾ cup).

Per serving: CALORIES 136; FAT 4.7g (sat 2.1g, mono 1.3g, poly 0.1g); PROTEIN 17.3g; CARB 8.2g; FIBER 1.8g; CHOL 40mg; IRON 1.9mg; SODIUM 597mg; CALC 25mg

Jalapeño Corn Bread Mini Muffins

prep: 9 minutes • **cook:** 17 minutes   *PointsPlus* value per serving: 3

  ¾ cup self-rising white cornmeal mix
  ½ cup nonfat buttermilk
  2 tablespoons minced seeded jalapeño pepper
  1½ tablespoons canola oil
  1 large egg
Cooking spray

1. Preheat oven to 425°.
2. Lightly spoon cornmeal mix into measuring cups; level with a knife, and place in a large bowl. Combine buttermilk, jalapeño pepper, canola oil, and egg in a small bowl. Pour buttermilk mixture into cornmeal mix; stir just until combined. Spoon batter into 12 miniature muffin cups coated with cooking spray.
3. Bake at 425° for 17 minutes or until lightly browned. Remove from pans immediately; serve warm. **Yield:** 6 servings (serving size: 2 mini muffins).

Per serving: CALORIES 127; FAT 4.8g (sat 0.5g, mono 2.5g, poly 1.1g); PROTEIN 3.7g; CARB 17.4g; FIBER 1.3g; CHOL 30mg; IRON 1.2mg; SODIUM 312mg; CALC 93mg

Egg Drop Soup

prep: 3 minutes • **cook:** 15 minutes   *PointsPlus* value per serving: 3

You can make this Chinese takeout favorite at home, easily—and with much less sodium.

2	cups shredded cooked chicken breast
½	teaspoon freshly ground black pepper
1	(32-ounce) container fat-free, lower-sodium chicken broth
¼	cup water
2½	tablespoons cornstarch
1	large egg, lightly beaten
½	cup chopped green onions (optional)

1. Combine first 3 ingredients in a large saucepan. Bring to a boil over medium-high heat. Cover and simmer 5 minutes.

2. Combine ¼ cup water and cornstarch in a small bowl. Add cornstarch mixture to broth mixture, stirring constantly with a whisk. Bring to a boil; cook, stirring constantly, 1 minute or until soup thickens slightly. Add egg to broth mixture in a slow, steady stream, stirring constantly with a wooden spoon. Remove from heat, and stir in onions, if desired. **Yield:** 5 servings (serving size: about 1 cup).

Per serving: CALORIES 136; FAT 3g (sat 0.9g, mono 1.1g, poly 0.6g); PROTEIN 21.4g; CARB 4.8g; FIBER 0.1g; CHOL 90mg; IRON 0.8mg; SODIUM 578mg; CALC 15mg

Menu
PointsPlus value
per serving: 6

Egg Drop Soup

1 low-fat frozen vegetable egg roll
PointsPlus value
per serving: 3

Game Plan

1. Preheat oven for egg rolls.

2. Shred chicken, and chop onion.

3. While egg rolls bake:
• Combine and heat soup ingredients.

---

pictured on page 43

Chicken Pasta Soup

prep: 2 minutes • **cook:** 22 minutes   *PointsPlus* value per serving: 4

	Cooking spray
1	cup matchstick-cut carrots
¼	teaspoon freshly ground black pepper
2	(6-ounce) skinless, boneless chicken breast halves, cut into bite-sized pieces
1	(8-ounce) container refrigerated prechopped celery, onion, and bell pepper mix
7	cups fat-free, lower-sodium chicken broth
1	cup uncooked whole-wheat rotini (corkscrew pasta)

1. Heat a Dutch oven over medium-high heat. Coat pan with cooking spray. Add carrots and next 3 ingredients; cook 6 minutes or until chicken begins to brown and vegetables are tender, stirring frequently. Add broth; bring to a boil. Add pasta, reduce heat to medium, and cook 8 minutes or until pasta is done. **Yield:** 6 servings (serving size: 1½ cups).

Per serving: CALORIES 156; FAT 3g (sat 0.6g, mono 0.6g, poly 0.4g); PROTEIN 20.4g; CARB 12.8g; FIBER 2.8g; CHOL 40mg; IRON 1.4mg; SODIUM 723mg; CALC 27mg

Menu
PointsPlus value
per serving: 8

Chicken Pasta Soup

Corn and Zucchini Muffins (page 160)
PointsPlus value
per serving: 4

Game Plan

1. Preheat oven for muffins.

2. Shred zucchini, and make muffin batter.

3. While muffins bake:
• Brown chicken and vegetables.
• Add pasta, and cook until done.

pictured on page 42

Southwestern Chicken and White Bean Soup

Menu
PointsPlus value per serving: 6

Southwestern Chicken and White Bean Soup

1 ounce baked tortilla chips
PointsPlus value per serving: 3

Game Plan

1. Shred chicken.

2. Rinse, drain, and mash beans.

3. While soup simmers:
  • Chop cilantro.
  • Measure chips.

prep: 2 minutes • **cook:** 16 minutes   *PointsPlus* value per serving: 3

> 2 cups shredded cooked chicken breast
> 1 tablespoon 40%-less-sodium taco seasoning
> Cooking spray
> 2 (14.5-ounce) cans fat-free, lower-sodium chicken broth
> 1 (15.5-ounce) can cannellini beans or other white beans, rinsed and drained
> ½ cup green salsa
> ¼ teaspoon freshly ground black pepper
> Light sour cream (optional)
> Chopped fresh cilantro (optional)

1. Combine chicken and taco seasoning; toss well to coat. Heat a large saucepan over medium-high heat. Coat pan with cooking spray. Add chicken; sauté 2 minutes or until chicken is lightly browned. Add broth, scraping pan to loosen browned bits.
2. Place beans in a small bowl; mash until only a few whole beans remain. Add beans, salsa, and pepper to pan, stirring well. Bring to a boil. Reduce heat; simmer 10 minutes or until slightly thick. Serve with sour cream and cilantro, if desired. **Yield:** 6 servings (serving size: 1 cup).

Per serving: CALORIES 134; FAT 3g (sat 0.5g, mono 0.6g, poly 0.5g); PROTEIN 18g; CARB 8.5g; FIBER 1.8g; CHOL 40mg; IRON 1.1mg; SODIUM 623mg; CALC 22mg

Creamy Chicken and Corn Chowder

Menu
PointsPlus value per serving: 8

Creamy Chicken and Corn Chowder

1 medium apple, cut into slices
PointsPlus value per serving: 0

Game Plan

1. Thaw corn.

2. Chop cooked chicken.

3. While soup simmers:
  • Cut apples.

prep: 5 minutes • **cook:** 15 minutes   *PointsPlus* value per serving: 8

Knock the chill off a cold winter's night with this simple yet satisfying homemade soup. Convenience items from your grocery store will help you prepare this recipe in minutes.

> 2 cups chopped roasted chicken breast
> 1 cup frozen extra-sweet whole-kernel corn
> 2 cups fat-free, lower-sodium chicken broth
> 1 (20-ounce) package frozen cream-style corn, thawed
> 1 (10-ounce) package frozen vegetable seasoning blend

1. Combine all ingredients in a Dutch oven. Bring to a boil; cover, reduce heat, and simmer 10 minutes, stirring occasionally. Serve immediately. **Yield:** 4 servings (serving size: 1¾ cups).

Per serving: CALORIES 316; FAT 2.9g (sat 0.8g, mono 1.0g, poly 0.7g); PROTEIN 26.6g; CARB 42.7g; FIBER 4.3g; CHOL 60mg; IRON 1.3mg; SODIUM 839mg; CALC 37mg

Blackened Salmon Sandwiches with Cucumber-Ranch Dressing

prep: 8 minutes • **cook:** 9 minutes   *PointsPlus* value per serving: 11

This sophisticated-looking sandwich is easy to make. Cucumber dressing is a cool complement to the spicy fish.

1½ tablespoons salt-free blackened redfish seasoning blend
 4 (4-ounce) skinless tail-end salmon fillets (about ½ inch thick)
 ¼ teaspoon salt
Olive oil–flavored cooking spray
 ½ cup grated English cucumber, pressed between paper towels
     and squeezed dry
 ⅓ cup light ranch dressing
 1 (12-ounce) loaf French bread (about 12 inches long)
 4 green leaf lettuce leaves
 ¼ cup thinly sliced English cucumber

1. Rub seasoning over fish; sprinkle with salt. Heat a large nonstick skillet over medium heat; coat pan with cooking spray. Add fillets. Cook 4 minutes on each side or until fish flakes easily when tested with a fork or until desired degree of doneness.

2. While fish cooks, combine grated cucumber and dressing. Slice bread in half lengthwise; cut into 4 portions. On bottom half of each portion, place 1 lettuce leaf, 1 salmon fillet, 3 cucumber slices, and 2 tablespoons cucumber-ranch dressing. Top with remaining half of bread. **Yield:** 4 servings (serving size: 1 sandwich).

Note: To reduce the *PointsPlus* value, reserve top half of bread portion for another use and serve sandwich open-faced. When served this way, the *PointsPlus* value is 8.

Per serving: CALORIES 434; FAT 11.8g (sat 2.1g, mono 3.8g, poly 2.1g); PROTEIN 32.9g; CARB 48.4g; FIBER 2g; CHOL 58mg; IRON 3mg; SODIUM 875mg; CALC 157mg

Menu
PointsPlus value
per serving: 11

**Blackened Salmon
Sandwiches with
Cucumber-Ranch Dressing**

Baby carrots
PointsPlus value
per serving: 0

Game Plan

1. While skillet heats:
• Grate cucumber.
• Season fish.

2. While fish blackens:
• Combine cucumber
  and dressing.

3. Assemble sandwiches.

Shrimp Rolls

prep: 10 minutes

PointsPlus value per serving: 6

1 small lemon
¼ cup light mayonnaise
2 tablespoons chopped green onion tops
½ cup finely chopped celery
¾ pound chopped cooked shrimp
4 (1.5-ounce) white-wheat hot dog buns
4 Boston lettuce leaves

1. Grate ½ teaspoon lemon rind from lemon. Squeeze lemon to measure 1½ table-spoons juice. Combine lemon rind, juice, mayonnaise, and green onions in a large bowl. Add celery and shrimp; toss gently.
2. Top each hot dog bun with 1 lettuce leaf. Spoon shrimp mixture onto lettuce leaves. Serve immediately. **Yield:** 4 servings (serving size: 1 sandwich).

Per serving: CALORIES 220; FAT 7.4g (sat 1g, mono 0.7g, poly 1.3g); PROTEIN 23.1g; CARB 20.7g; FIBER 4.5g; CHOL 171mg; IRON 5.5mg; SODIUM 514mg; CALC 296mg

Menu
PointsPlus value per serving: 6

Shrimp Rolls

1 cup strawberry slices
PointsPlus value per serving: 0

Game Plan

1. Chop green onions, celery, and shrimp.

2. Combine shrimp mixture.

3. Slice strawberries.

4. Assemble rolls.

Greek Salad–Stuffed Pitas

Create a portable lunch by spooning tangy Greek salad into pita-bread pockets.

prep: 20 minutes

PointsPlus value per serving: 7

2 cups chopped plum tomato (about 5)
1 cup chopped peeled cucumber (about 1 small)
¼ cup chopped pitted kalamata olives
2 tablespoons chopped fresh dill
1 tablespoon fresh lemon juice
2 teaspoons extra-virgin olive oil
½ teaspoon freshly ground black pepper
¼ teaspoon salt
4 (6-inch) onion pitas, cut in half
8 small curly leaf lettuce leaves
2 ounces crumbled feta cheese (about ½ cup)

1. Combine first 8 ingredients in a large bowl; toss to combine. Line each pita half with a lettuce leaf. Spoon about ⅓ cup tomato mixture into each pita half, and sprinkle with 1 tablespoon cheese. **Yield:** 4 servings (serving size: 2 pita halves).

Per serving: CALORIES 280; FAT 9g (sat 3.5g, mono 4.3g, poly 0.7g); PROTEIN 11g; CARB 40g; FIBER 2.5g; CHOL 17mg; IRON 3.5mg; SODIUM 672mg; CALC 153mg

Menu
PointsPlus value per serving: 7

Greek Salad–Stuffed Pitas

1 cup grapes
PointsPlus value per serving: 0

Game Plan

1. Chop vegetables, olives, and dill.

2. Split and line pita halves with lettuce.

3. Assemble sandwiches.

pictured on page 44

Mushroom and Swiss Paninis

prep: 6 minutes • **cook:** 10 minutes   *PointsPlus* value per serving: 8

Crusty grilled bread surrounds melted cheese and mushrooms, making this grown-up grilled cheese irresistible.

Olive oil–flavored cooking spray
2   tablespoons minced shallots
1   (8-ounce) package sliced baby portobello mushrooms
1   teaspoon minced fresh thyme
¼   teaspoon salt
¼   teaspoon freshly ground black pepper
1   garlic clove, minced
¼   cup light mayonnaise
8   (0.9-ounce) slices Italian bread
8   (0.75-ounce) slices reduced-fat Swiss cheese

1. Heat a large nonstick skillet over medium-high heat; coat pan with cooking spray. Add shallots; cook 1 minute or until tender. Add mushrooms; cook 5 minutes, stirring occasionally. Add thyme and next 3 ingredients; cook 1 minute, stirring occasionally. Remove pan from heat.

2. Preheat panini grill.

3. Spread 1½ teaspoons mayonnaise on each bread slice; top 4 bread slices with 1 cheese slice, cutting cheese to fit, if needed. Top each with one-fourth of mushroom mixture, 1 cheese slice, and 1 bread slice. Coat sandwiches with cooking spray. Place sandwiches on panini grill, and cook 3 to 4 minutes or until golden and cheese melts. **Yield:** 4 servings (serving size: 1 sandwich).

Note: If you don't have a panini grill, place sandwiches in a large nonstick skillet over medium heat. Place a piece of foil over sandwiches; top with a heavy skillet. Cook 2 to 3 minutes on each side or until golden and cheese melts.

Per serving: CALORIES 300; FAT 10g (sat 4.3g, mono 1.0g, poly 0.8g); PROTEIN 21.3g; CARB 31.6g; FIBER 2.3g; CHOL 23mg; IRON 2mg; SODIUM 656mg; CALC 504mg

Menu
PointsPlus value per serving: 8

Mushroom and Swiss Paninis

1 cup blueberries
PointsPlus value per serving: 0

Game Plan

1. Sauté shallots and mushrooms.

2. While grill heats:
• Assemble sandwiches.
• Measure blueberries.

3. Grill paninis.

Apple and Cheddar Grilled Cheese

prep: 6 minutes • **cook:** 4 minutes   *PointsPlus* value per serving: 8

Give a classic grilled cheese sandwich a modern flair by combining sweet, crisp apple slices with cheddar cheese.

2   tablespoons stone-ground Dijon mustard
2   tablespoons light mayonnaise
8   (1-ounce) slices multigrain Italian bread
4   ounces reduced-fat shredded cheddar cheese (about 1 cup)
1   medium Gala apple, cored and sliced
Cooking spray

1. Combine mustard and mayonnaise in a small bowl. Spread onto bread slices. Top 4 bread slices with 2 tablespoons cheese, apple slices, 2 tablespoons cheese, and remaining bread slices. Coat both sides of sandwiches with cooking spray.
2. Heat a large nonstick skillet over medium heat. Coat pan with cooking spray. Cook sandwiches 2 to 3 minutes on each side or until golden brown and cheese melts. **Yield:** 4 servings (serving size: 1 sandwich).

Per serving: CALORIES 311; FAT 11g (sat 4.9g, mono 2.5g, poly 2.4g); PROTEIN 12.8g; CARB 36.7g; FIBER 3.1g; CHOL 23mg; IRON 2mg; SODIUM 784mg; CALC 255mg

Menu
PointsPlus value
per serving: 8

Apple and Cheddar
Grilled Cheese

1 medium orange,
cut into wedges
PointsPlus value
per serving: 0

Game Plan

1. While skillet heats:
  • Core and slice apple.
  • Assemble sandwiches.

2. Cook sandwiches.

3. Cut oranges.

Open-Faced Ham and Swiss Sandwiches

prep: 10 minutes • **cook:** 2 minutes   *PointsPlus* value per serving: 6

This meaty indulgence will satisfy your craving for a deli sandwich.

8   teaspoons Dijon mustard
4   (1-ounce) slices rye bread
½   pound thinly sliced deli ham
8   precooked bacon slices
4   (⅛-inch-thick) slices tomato
4   (⅝-ounce) slices Swiss cheese

1. Preheat broiler.
2. Spread 2 teaspoons mustard over each bread slice. Divide ham among bread slices. Top each with 2 bacon slices, 1 tomato slice, and 1 cheese slice. Place sandwiches on a baking sheet; broil 2 minutes or until cheese melts. Serve immediately. **Yield:** 4 servings (serving size: 1 open-faced sandwich).

Per serving: CALORIES 267; FAT 11.1g (sat 4.6g, mono 4.1g, poly 1.8g); PROTEIN 19.2g; CARB 17g; FIBER 1.3g; CHOL 54mg; IRON 1.2mg; SODIUM 955mg; CALC 61mg

Menu
PointsPlus value
per serving: 10

Open-Faced Ham and
Swiss Sandwiches

1 ounce baked
sweet potato chips
PointsPlus value
per serving: 4

Game Plan

1. Preheat broiler.

2. Slice tomato.

3. Assemble sandwiches,
and broil.

Curried Chicken Salad Sandwiches

prep: 19 minutes • **cook:** 3 minutes   *PointsPlus* value per serving: 9

If you don't want to make all eight sandwiches at once, simply keep the chicken salad in the refrigerator, and assemble the sandwiches as desired. Or if you prefer to eat chicken salad without the bread, a ½-cup portion has a *PointsPlus* value of 5.

- ½ cup light mayonnaise
- ¼ cup plain low-fat yogurt
- 1 teaspoon curry powder
- 1 teaspoon fresh lemon juice
- ½ teaspoon salt
- 4 cups shredded cooked chicken breast
- ½ cup seedless red grapes, halved
- ½ cup chopped walnuts, toasted
- ⅓ cup diced red onion
- 1 (8-ounce) can pineapple tidbits in juice, drained
- 16 slices whole-wheat double-fiber bread
- 8 lettuce leaves

1. Combine first 5 ingredients in a large bowl. Add chicken and next 4 ingredients; stir well to combine.

2. Top each of 8 bread slices with ½ cup chicken salad. Top each with 1 lettuce leaf and 1 bread slice. **Yield:** 8 servings (serving size: 1 sandwich).

Per serving: CALORIES 321; FAT 14.1g (sat 2.1g, mono 2.8g, poly 6.7g); PROTEIN 32.4g; CARB 28.4g; FIBER 10.9g; CHOL 65mg; IRON 4.1mg; SODIUM 626mg; CALC 339mg

---

Menu
PointsPlus value
per serving: 10

Curried Chicken Salad Sandwiches

Melon Salad with Lavender-Honey Dressing (page 80)
PointsPlus value
per serving: 1

Game Plan

1. Halve grapes.

2. Chop walnuts and onion; shred chicken.

3. Combine salad ingredients, and toss fruit with dressing.

4. Assemble sandwiches.

Menu
PointsPlus value
per serving: 8

Sesame-Ginger Chicken Wraps
with Peanut Sauce

1 cup pineapple cubes
PointsPlus value
per serving: 0

Game Plan

1. Shred cabbage.

2. While skillet heats:
   • Slice cucumber.
   • Marinate cucumber in vinegar.
   • Season chicken.

3. Cook chicken.

4. Prepare Peanut Sauce.

5. Assemble sandwiches.

Sesame-Ginger Chicken Wraps with Peanut Sauce

prep: 23 minutes • **cook:** 9 minutes   *PointsPlus* value per serving: 8

    2   cups thinly sliced cucumber (about 1 large)
    ½   cup rice wine vinegar
    2   (6-ounce) skinless, boneless chicken breast halves,
        cut in half horizontally
    2   teaspoons canola oil
    1½ tablespoons sesame seeds
    1   teaspoon ground ginger
    ¼   teaspoon salt
  Cooking spray
    2   cups shredded napa (Chinese) cabbage
    4   (1.9-ounce) multigrain sandwich wraps
  Peanut Sauce

1. Combine cucumber slices and vinegar in a medium bowl; let stand, stirring often.
2. While cucumber stands, brush chicken with oil; sprinkle with sesame seeds, ginger, and salt, pressing to adhere. Heat a large nonstick skillet over medium-high heat. Coat pan with cooking spray. Add chicken; cook 3 minutes on each side or until done. Remove from heat; keep warm.
3. Place ½ cup cabbage and ½ cup cucumber slices on each wrap. Cut chicken into strips, and toss with Peanut Sauce. Arrange chicken over cucumber. Roll up; secure with wooden picks, if necessary. **Yield:** 4 servings (serving size: 1 wrap).

Per serving: CALORIES 307; FAT 11.7g (sat 1.2g, mono 2.4g, poly 3.6g); PROTEIN 32g; CARB 24.8g; FIBER 10.3g; CHOL 49mg; IRON 3.1mg; SODIUM 664mg; CALC 87mg

Peanut Sauce

prep: 5 minutes • **cook:** 3 minutes   *PointsPlus* value per serving: 2

    2   tablespoons water
    2   tablespoons natural-style creamy peanut butter
    1   teaspoon brown sugar
    1   teaspoon rice wine vinegar
    1   teaspoon lower-sodium soy sauce
    1   garlic clove, minced
  Dash of ground red pepper

1. Combine all ingredients in a small saucepan, stirring with a whisk. Bring to a boil over medium heat, and cook 1 minute. **Yield:** ¼ cup (serving size: 1 tablespoon).

Per serving: CALORIES 56; FAT 4g (sat 0.5g, mono 1.1g, poly 2.3g); PROTEIN 1.9g; CARB 3.2g; FIBER 0.5g; CHOL 0mg; IRON 0.2mg; SODIUM 78mg; CALC 2mg

Turkey Reubens

prep: 4 minutes • **cook:** 4 minutes per batch   *PointsPlus* value per serving: 8

  8 ounces thinly sliced lower-sodium smoked turkey breast
  8 (1-ounce) slices rye bread
  ¼ cup reduced-fat Thousand Island dressing
  ¾ cup canned Bavarian-style sauerkraut, drained
  4 (1-ounce) slices reduced-fat, reduced-sodium Swiss cheese
    Cooking spray

1. Divide turkey among 4 bread slices, and spread 1 tablespoon dressing over turkey on each sandwich. Top each with 3 tablespoons sauerkraut, 1 cheese slice, and a bread slice. Coat tops of sandwiches with cooking spray.
2. Heat a large nonstick skillet over medium heat. Place 2 sandwiches, coated sides down, in pan. Cook 2 to 3 minutes or until bread is golden and cheese begins to melt. Coat sandwiches with cooking spray; turn sandwiches. Cook 2 to 3 minutes or until bread is golden and cheese melts. Repeat procedure with remaining sandwiches. Serve immediately. **Yield:** 4 servings (serving: 1 sandwich).

Per serving: CALORIES 327; FAT 10g (sat 4.5g, mono 2.8g, poly 1.0g); PROTEIN 22.8g; CARB 35.8g; FIBER 4.4g; CHOL 32mg; IRON 2.5mg; SODIUM 999mg; CALC 297mg

pictured on page 45

Easy Pulled Pork Sandwiches

prep: 8 minutes • **cook:** 1 hour   *PointsPlus* value per serving: 6

  ½ cup finely chopped onion
  ¼ cup finely chopped celery
  ¼ cup barbecue sauce
  1 teaspoon garlic powder
  1 teaspoon ground cumin
  1 (1-pound) pork tenderloin, trimmed and cut into 4 pieces
  1 (14.5-ounce) can diced tomatoes, undrained
  6 (1.6-ounce) light wheat hamburger buns, toasted

1. Combine first 7 ingredients in a medium saucepan over medium-high heat; bring to a boil. Cover, reduce heat, and simmer 55 minutes. Remove from heat. Remove pork from sauce; shred pork. Return pork to sauce.
2. Place about ⅓ cup pork mixture on bottom half of each bun; top with top halves of buns. **Yield:** 6 servings (serving size: 1 sandwich).

Per serving: CALORIES 200; FAT 4g (sat 0.9g, mono 0g, poly 0g); PROTEIN 20.7g; CARB 29.8g; FIBER 6.3g; CHOL 42mg; IRON 2.9mg; SODIUM 405mg; CALC 71mg

---

Menu
PointsPlus value per serving: 11

Turkey Reubens

1 ounce baked potato chips
PointsPlus value per serving: 3

Game Plan

1. While skillet heats:
 • Drain sauerkraut.
 • Assemble sandwiches.

2. Cook Reubens.

3. Serve hot with chips.

Menu
PointsPlus value per serving: 9

Easy Pulled Pork Sandwiches

Creamy Ranch-Style Coleslaw (page 81)
PointsPlus value per serving: 3

Game Plan

1. Chop vegetables for pork.

2. While pork mixture simmers:
 • Combine slaw ingredients, and chill.
 • Toast buns.

3. Shred pork before serving.

Menu
PointsPlus value
per serving: 9

Steak and Feta Hoagies

1 peach
PointsPlus value
per serving: 0

Game Plan

1. While oven preheats:
• Slice vegetables.
• Hollow out rolls.

2. While steak cooks:
• Toss greens mixture.

3. Assemble hoagies.

4. Wash peaches.

Steak and Feta Hoagies

prep: 10 minutes • **cook:** 7 minutes • **other:** 3 minutes

PointsPlus value per serving: 9

4   (3-ounce) whole-wheat hoagie rolls
12   ounces boneless lean sirloin steak
1   teaspoon chili powder
½   teaspoon coarsely ground black pepper
Cooking spray
3   cups mixed baby greens
2   ounces crumbled reduced-fat feta cheese (about ½ cup)
½   cup thinly sliced red bell pepper
¼   cup thinly sliced red onion
¼   cup fat-free red wine vinaigrette

1. Preheat oven to 350°.
2. Halve hoagie rolls horizontally. Hollow out top and bottom halves of rolls, leaving a ½-inch border. Reserve torn bread for another use. Place rolls on a baking sheet, cut sides down, and bake at 350° for 5 minutes or until toasted. Remove from oven, and set aside.
3. While rolls toast, sprinkle both sides of steak with chili powder and black pepper. Heat a large nonstick skillet over medium-high heat; coat pan with cooking spray. Add steak, and cook 2 to 3 minutes on each side or until desired degree of doneness. Remove pan from heat, and let steak stand in pan 3 minutes.
4. While steak stands, combine greens and next 4 ingredients in a medium bowl, tossing gently.
5. Cut steak diagonally across grain into thin slices. Top bottom half of each roll with steak slices; drizzle any remaining juices from pan over each. Top each with one-fourth of salad mixture and top half of roll. **Yield:** 4 servings (serving size: 1 sandwich).

Per serving: CALORIES 346; FAT 9.9g (sat 3.6g, mono 0.8g, poly 1.4g); PROTEIN 27.9g; CARB 38.5g; FIBER 6.6g; CHOL 55mg; IRON 3.8mg; SODIUM 794mg; CALC 139mg

Salads

PointsPlus value per serving: 1
Melon Salad with Lavender-Honey
  Dressing | page 80
Crunchy Coleslaw with Spring Peas | page 81
Caesar Romaine with Black Bread Croutons | page 85

PointsPlus value per serving: 2
Cucumber Salad with Feta Cheese | page 82
Sweet Onion Salad | page 82
Carrot Salad with Grapes | page 83
Spring Greens with Hot Sauce Dressing | page 84
Rustic Mediterranean Tomato Salad | page 84
Lemony Romaine Wedges with Cucumber | page 85
Pear, Strawberry, and Spinach Salad | page 86
Arugula, Pear, and Gorgonzola Salad | page 87

PointsPlus value per serving: 3
Fresh Fruit Salad with Lemon Cream | page 80
Creamy Ranch-Style Coleslaw | page 81
Spicy Vegetable Salad with Pasta | page 86

PointsPlus value per serving: 4
Warm Fingerling Potato Salad | page 83
Lemony Bulgur Salad | page 87

PointsPlus value per serving: 5
Tex-Mex Layered Salad | page 88
Chef's Salad with Creamy Dijon
  Dressing | page 94

PointsPlus value per serving: 6
Italian Cobb Salad | page 93

PointsPlus value per serving: 7
Tropical Shrimp Salad | page 91
Portobellos and Flank Steak over
  Greens | page 92
Orecchiette and Roasted Chicken
  Salad | page 93

PointsPlus value per serving: 8
Salmon Pasta Salad with Lemon and
  Capers | page 89

PointsPlus value per serving: 9
Grilled Salmon Salade Niçoise | page 90

Menu
PointsPlus value
per serving: 7

**Fresh Fruit Salad
with Lemon Cream**

**Blueberry–Brown Sugar
Muffins (page 161)**
PointsPlus value
per serving: 4

Game Plan

1. Prepare muffin batter.

2. While muffins bake:
   • Cut fruit.
   • Grate rind, and chop mint.

3. Toss fruit with yogurt
mixture.

Fresh Fruit Salad with Lemon Cream

prep: 22 minutes

PointsPlus value per serving: 3

Extra lemon cream is also great spooned over low-fat pound cake.

1   tablespoon brown sugar
2   tablespoons reduced-fat sour cream
½   teaspoon grated fresh lemon rind
1   (6-ounce) carton lemon low-fat yogurt
2   cups chopped cantaloupe (about ½ medium)
1   cup pineapple chunks
1   cup sliced strawberries
1   tablespoon chopped fresh mint
2   cubed peeled kiwifruit

1. Combine first 4 ingredients in a small bowl; cover and chill until ready to serve.
2. Combine cantaloupe and next 4 ingredients in a large bowl, tossing well to combine.
Divide fruit salad among 5 serving bowls; spoon lemon cream over each serving.
Yield: 5 servings (serving size: 1 cup fruit salad and 2 tablespoons lemon cream).

Per serving: CALORIES 117; FAT 1.4g (sat 0.7g, mono 0.2g, poly 0.2g); PROTEIN 2.5g; CARB 25.5g; FIBER 2.1g; CHOL 4mg; IRON 0.5mg; SODIUM 31mg; CALC 74mg

Menu
PointsPlus value
per serving: 10

**Melon Salad with Lavender-
Honey Dressing**

**Curried Chicken Salad
Sandwiches (page 75)**
PointsPlus value
per serving: 9

Game Plan

1. Halve grapes.

2. Chop walnuts and onion;
shred chicken.

3. Combine salad ingredients,
and toss fruit with dressing.

4. Assemble sandwiches.

Melon Salad with Lavender-Honey Dressing

prep: 4 minutes

PointsPlus value per serving: 1

**Choose this sweet and tangy melon salad to accompany any grilled
chicken entrée. Using prechopped melon from the produce section of
the grocery store will speed preparation immensely.**

1   tablespoon chopped fresh mint
1   tablespoon fresh lime juice
1   teaspoon lavender honey
2   cups mixed melon

1. Combine first 3 ingredients in a small bowl. Pour dressing over melon, tossing to
coat. **Yield:** 4 servings (serving size: ½ cup).

Per serving: CALORIES 36; FAT 0.2g (sat 0g, mono 0g, poly 0.1g); PROTEIN 0.6g; CARB 9g; FIBER 0.8g; CHOL 0mg; IRON 0.3mg; SODIUM 15mg; CALC 10mg

Crunchy Coleslaw with Spring Peas

prep: 9 minutes   *PointsPlus* value per serving: 1

Using frozen peas saves time and lets you prepare this recipe year-round. Opt for blanched early spring peas when available.

4	cups packaged coleslaw
½	cup frozen green peas, thawed
½	cup chopped yellow bell pepper
½	cup matchstick-cut carrots
¼	cup finely chopped onion
2	tablespoons sugar
3	tablespoons cider vinegar
1½	teaspoons canola oil
¼	teaspoon salt

1. Place all ingredients in a large bowl; toss gently to coat. Serve immediately.
Yield: 8 servings (serving size: about ⅔ cup).

Per serving: CALORIES 43; FAT 0.9g (sat 0.1g, mono 0.5g, poly 0.3g); PROTEIN 1g; CARB 7.8g; FIBER 1.5g; CHOL 0mg; IRON 0.2mg; SODIUM 91mg; CALC 7mg

Menu
PointsPlus value per serving: 5

Crunchy Coleslaw with Spring Peas

4 ounces grilled chicken tenders
PointsPlus value per serving: 4

Game Plan

1. While grill heats:
   • Thaw peas.
   • Chop pepper and onion.

2. Grill chicken.

3. Toss slaw ingredients.

Creamy Ranch-Style Coleslaw

prep: 7 minutes   *PointsPlus* value per serving: 3

This creamy slaw is best after chilling about two hours in the refrigerator.

4	cups packaged coleslaw
⅓	cup light mayonnaise
¼	cup nonfat buttermilk
1	teaspoon salt-free onion and herb seasoning blend
¼	teaspoon salt
⅛	teaspoon freshly ground pepper

1. Place coleslaw in a large bowl. Combine mayonnaise and next 4 ingredients in a bowl, stirring well with a whisk. Pour dressing over slaw; toss well. Chill until ready to serve. **Yield:** 4 servings (serving size: 1 cup).

Per serving: CALORIES 90; FAT 6.6g (sat 1g, mono 1.2g, poly 2.7g); PROTEIN 1.6g; CARB 6.7g; FIBER 1.8g; CHOL 7mg; IRON 0.4mg; SODIUM 331mg; CALC 48mg

Menu
PointsPlus value per serving: 9

Creamy Ranch-Style Coleslaw

Easy Pulled Pork Sandwiches (page 77)
PointsPlus value per serving: 6

Game Plan

1. Chop vegetables for pork.

2. While pork mixture simmers:
   • Combine slaw ingredients, and chill.
   • Toast buns.

3. Shred pork before serving.

Cucumber Salad with Feta Cheese

Menu
PointsPlus value per serving: 6

Cucumber Salad with Feta Cheese

6 ounces grilled tilapia
PointsPlus value per serving: 4

Game Plan

1. Slice vegetables.

2. Toss cucumber mixture, and chill.

3. Grill fish.

4. Top cucumber mixture with cheese.

prep: 18 minutes • **other:** 3 hours   *PointsPlus* value per serving: 2

Jalapeño pepper and feta cheese contribute a little heat and extra tang to a traditional marinated cucumber salad.

- ½   cup cider vinegar
- 1   tablespoon sugar
- 2   tablespoons water
- 1   tablespoon canola oil
- ¼   teaspoon salt
- ¼   teaspoon freshly ground black pepper
- 4   cups thinly sliced peeled cucumber
- ½   cup vertically sliced red onion
- 1   jalapeño pepper, seeded and chopped
- 1   ounce crumbled feta cheese (about ¼ cup)

1. Combine first 6 ingredients in a medium bowl, stirring with a whisk until blended. Add cucumber, onion, and jalapeño; toss to coat. Cover and chill at least 3 hours. Sprinkle with cheese. **Yield:** 6 servings (serving size: about ¾ cup cucumber mixture and 2 teaspoons cheese).

Per serving: CALORIES 65; FAT 3.8g (sat 1.1g, mono 1.8g, poly 0.7g); PROTEIN 1.6g; CARB 5.5g; FIBER 0.9g; CHOL 6mg; IRON 0.3mg; SODIUM 170mg; CALC 48mg

Sweet Onion Salad

Menu
PointsPlus value per serving: 4

Sweet Onion Salad

1 ounce warm ciabatta bread
PointsPlus value per serving: 2

Game Plan

1. Slice vegetables.

2. Preheat oven to warm bread.

3. Toss salad ingredients.

4. Toast bread.

prep: 8 minutes   *PointsPlus* value per serving: 2

Grape tomatoes, which are actually baby plum tomatoes, have a more intense sweetness than cherry tomatoes. For the best flavor, look for grape tomatoes that are no more than 1 inch in diameter.

- 1½   cups grape tomatoes, halved
- 1½   cups English cucumber slices (about 1 small)
- 1   cup vertically sliced sweet onion
- ⅓   cup sweet Vidalia onion vinaigrette

1. Combine tomatoes, cucumber, and onion in a bowl. Add dressing; toss well. **Yield:** 4 servings (serving size: 1 cup).

Per serving: CALORIES 85; FAT 3.1g (sat 0.4g, mono 0.6g, poly 1.6g); PROTEIN 1.1g; CARB 14.4g; FIBER 1.8g; CHOL 0mg; IRON 0.2mg; SODIUM 85mg; CALC 25mg

Carrot Salad with Grapes

prep: 8 minutes • other: 5 minutes   *PointsPlus* value per serving: 2

To get a moist, tender salad, we recommend shredding the carrots yourself.

- ¼ cup light mayonnaise
- 2 tablespoons orange juice
- 1 teaspoon sugar
- ⅔ cup seedless red grapes, halved
- 6 medium carrots, shredded

1. Combine first 3 ingredients in a large bowl, stirring with a whisk until blended. Add grapes and carrot, tossing well to coat. Let stand 5 minutes. **Yield:** 4 servings (serving size: ¾ cup).

Per serving: CALORIES 113; FAT 5.3g (sat 1.6g, mono 0.9g, poly 0.6g); PROTEIN 1.1g; CARB 16.4g; FIBER 2.8g; CHOL 5mg; IRON 0.4mg; SODIUM 184mg; CALC 34mg

Menu
PointsPlus value
per serving: 5

Carrot Salad with Grapes

1 (6-ounce) carton vanilla fat-free Greek yogurt
PointsPlus value
per serving: 3

Game Plan

1. Shred carrots.
2. Halve grapes.
3. Combine salad ingredients.

Warm Fingerling Potato Salad

prep: 10 minutes • cook: 20 minutes   *PointsPlus* value per serving: 4

Fingerling potatoes are not a specific variety of potato. Instead, they are immature potatoes with a long, thin shape. They can be white, red-skinned, or yellow-fleshed, and vary in texture from waxy to starchy. In this recipe, you can substitute small red potatoes.

- 10 fingerling potatoes, cut into ⅛-inch-thick slices (about 3 cups)
- ½ cup fat-free balsamic vinaigrette
- 1 tablespoon chopped fresh basil
- 2 teaspoons whole-grain mustard
- ¼ teaspoon salt
- ¼ teaspoon freshly ground black pepper
- 4 ounces goat cheese (about ½ cup), crumbled

1. Preheat broiler.
2. Place potato in a medium saucepan; cover with an inch of water. Bring to a boil. Reduce heat; simmer 5 minutes or until tender. Drain.
3. While potato cooks, combine balsamic vinaigrette and next 4 ingredients in a small bowl, stirring with a whisk.
4. Pour mixture over hot potato, tossing to coat. Spoon potato mixture into an 11 x 7–inch glass or ceramic baking dish; sprinkle with goat cheese.
5. Broil 5 minutes or until cheese is lightly browned. **Yield:** 6 servings (serving size: ½ cup).

Per serving: CALORIES 146; FAT 5.7g (sat 3.9g, mono 1.3g, poly 0.2g); PROTEIN 5.7g; CARB 18g; FIBER 1.2g; CHOL 15mg; IRON 0.9mg; SODIUM 487mg; CALC 63mg

Menu
PointsPlus value
per serving: 9

Warm Fingerling Potato Salad

Soy-Lime Lamb Chops (page 111)
PointsPlus value
per serving: 5

Game Plan

1. Marinate lamb chops.
2. Slice potatoes.
3. While potatoes cook:
   • Preheat grill.
   • Whisk dressing together.
4. Broil potatoes while chops are on grill.

Spring Greens with Hot Sauce Dressing

prep: 3 minutes   *PointsPlus* value per serving: 2

Olive oil can be kept at room temperature for up to six months, or if stored in the refrigerator, it should last up to one year. Chilled olive oil may appear slightly cloudy, but the cloudiness will disappear once it returns to room temperature.

- 1   (5-ounce) bag mixed baby lettuces
- 1½ tablespoons extra-virgin olive oil
- 2   teaspoons hot sauce
- 1½ tablespoons drained capers

1. Place mixed baby lettuces in a large bowl. Combine olive oil and hot sauce in a small bowl; stir with a whisk. Stir in capers. Pour dressing over lettuce, and toss well. Serve immediately. **Yield:** 4 servings (serving size: 1½ cups).

Per serving: CALORIES 52; FAT 5.1g (sat 0.7g, mono 3.7g, poly 0.6g); PROTEIN 0.5g; CARB 1.9g; FIBER 0.9g; CHOL 0mg; IRON 0.4mg; SODIUM 170mg; CALC 2mg

Rustic Mediterranean Tomato Salad

prep: 17 minutes • **other:** 2 hours   *PointsPlus* value per serving: 2

- 1   (14-ounce) can quartered artichoke hearts, drained
- 2   cups grape tomatoes, halved
- ¼   cup finely chopped red onion
- ¼   cup sliced pepperoncini peppers (about 6)
- 2   tablespoons chopped fresh parsley
- 2   tablespoons drained capers
- 1½   tablespoons chopped fresh basil leaves
- 1½   tablespoons cider vinegar
- ⅛   teaspoon salt
- 3   ounces part-skim mozzarella cheese (about ¾ cup), cut into ¼-inch cubes

1. Cut artichoke quarters in half lengthwise, if desired, and place in a large zip-top plastic bag. Add tomatoes and remaining ingredients. Seal bag; toss to coat. Chill 2 hours. **Yield:** 6 servings (serving size: ¾ cup).

Per serving: CALORIES 66; FAT 2.4g (sat 1.5g, mono 0.7g, poly 0.1g); PROTEIN 5.1g; CARB 6g; FIBER 0.9g; CHOL 8mg; IRON 1mg; SODIUM 433mg; CALC 105mg

pictured on page 47

Caesar Romaine with Black Bread Croutons

prep: 6 minutes • **cook:** 10 minutes   *PointsPlus* value per serving: 1

2   (0.8-ounce) slices pumpernickel or dark rye bread, cut into ½-inch cubes
¼   cup finely chopped red onion
1   (10-ounce) package torn hearts of romaine lettuce
⅓   cup nonfat buttermilk
2   tablespoons fat-free sour cream
1½   teaspoons anchovy paste
¼   teaspoon dried oregano
1   garlic clove, minced
¼   teaspoon coarsely ground black pepper

1. Preheat oven to 350°.
2. Arrange bread cubes in a single layer on a baking sheet. Bake at 350° for 10 minutes. Remove from oven, and cool completely.
3. While bread cubes bake, combine onion and lettuce in a large bowl. Set aside.
4. Combine buttermilk and next 4 ingredients in a medium bowl, stirring with a whisk until blended.
5. Add dressing and croutons to lettuce mixture; toss gently to coat. Sprinkle each serving with pepper, and serve immediately. **Yield:** 6 servings (serving size: 1 cup).

Per serving: CALORIES 43; FAT 0.4g (sat 0.1g, mono 0.1g, poly 0.2g); PROTEIN 2.4g; CARB 7.8g; FIBER 1.7g; CHOL 2mg; IRON 0.9mg; SODIUM 290mg; CALC 58mg

---

Menu
PointsPlus value
per serving: 3

Caesar Romaine with Black Bread Croutons

1 cup black bean soup
PointsPlus value
per serving: 2

Game Plan

1. While oven preheats:
 • Cut bread cubes.
 • Chop onion, and mince garlic.

2. While croutons bake:
 • Whisk dressing together.
 • Heat soup.

3. Toss salad.

Lemony Romaine Wedges with Cucumber

prep: 4 minutes   *PointsPlus* value per serving: 2

3   tablespoons fresh lemon juice
3   tablespoons olive oil
¼   teaspoon salt
¼   teaspoon freshly ground black pepper
3   heads romaine lettuce, halved lengthwise
2   cups thinly sliced pickling cucumber (about 2)

1. Combine first 4 ingredients in a small bowl, stirring with a whisk. Divide lettuce halves among 6 plates; sprinkle with cucumber slices, and drizzle with dressing. **Yield:** 6 servings (serving size: ½ romaine heart, ⅓ cup cucumber slices, and 1 tablespoon dressing).

Per serving: CALORIES 78; FAT 7g (sat 1g, mono 4.9g, poly 0.8g); PROTEIN 1g; CARB 3.8g; FIBER 1.6g; CHOL 0mg; IRON 0.7mg; SODIUM 102mg; CALC 27mg

---

Menu
PointsPlus value
per serving: 5

Lemony Romaine Wedges with Cucumber

1 ounce multigrain herbed pita chips
PointsPlus value
per serving: 3

Game Plan

1. Slice lettuce and cucumbers.

2. Whisk dressing together.

3. Assemble salad, and serve with chips.

Pear, Strawberry, and Spinach Salad

Menu
***PointsPlus* value per serving: 6**

Pear, Strawberry, and Spinach Salad

4 ounces skinless rotisserie chicken breast
***PointsPlus* value per serving: 4**

Game Plan

1. Cut strawberries and pear.

2. Separate breast meat from bone.

3. Toss salad.

4. Serve chicken with salad.

prep: 5 minutes   *PointsPlus* value per serving: 2

Strawberries are at their peak between the months of April and July. When purchasing strawberries, choose bright red, plump berries that still have the green caps attached.

    1   pear
   10   strawberries
    ¼   cup light balsamic vinaigrette
    1   (5- or 6-ounce) package fresh baby spinach
    Freshly ground black pepper (optional)

1. Core pear, and cut lengthwise into ¼-inch-thick slices; halve strawberries. Combine pear slices and strawberry halves with balsamic vinaigrette and spinach; toss gently. Sprinkle with black pepper, if desired. **Yield:** 4 servings (serving size: 1¾ cups).

Per serving: CALORIES 69; FAT 2.1g (sat 0.3g, mono 0.5g, poly 1.2g); PROTEIN 1.2g; CARB 12.9g; FIBER 3.6g; CHOL 0mg; IRON 1.2mg; SODIUM 292mg; CALC 33mg

---

pictured on page 48

Spicy Vegetable Salad with Pasta

Menu
***PointsPlus* value per serving: 3**

Spicy Vegetable Salad with Pasta

1 medium apple, sliced
***PointsPlus* value per serving: 0**

Game Plan

1. Cook pasta.

2. While pasta cooks:
   • Cut vegetables and cilantro.
   • Drain and slice olives.

3. Toss pasta mixture together.

4. Slice apples.

prep: 16 minutes • **cook:** 13 minutes • **other:** 15 minutes

PointsPlus value per serving: 3

    4   ounces uncooked multigrain rotini
    1   cup grape tomatoes, halved
    1   cup diced green bell pepper
    ¼   cup finely chopped green onions
    2   tablespoons chopped fresh cilantro
    ½   teaspoon grated fresh lemon rind
    2   tablespoons fresh lemon juice
    2   teaspoons extra-virgin olive oil
   12   queen-sized jalapeño-stuffed green olives, sliced

1. Cook pasta according to package directions, omitting salt and fat. Drain; rinse with cold water. Drain.
2. While pasta cooks, combine tomatoes and next 7 ingredients in a medium bowl. Add pasta; toss. Let stand 15 minutes. **Yield:** 6 servings (serving size: about ¾ cup).

Per serving: CALORIES 110; FAT 3.4g (sat 0.3g, mono 2.2g, poly 0.7g); PROTEIN 3g; CARB 18g; FIBER 1.5g; CHOL 0mg; IRON 0.8mg; SODIUM 255mg; CALC 12mg

Lemony Bulgur Salad

prep: 15 minutes • **cook:** 6 minutes • **other:** 2 hours and 30 minutes

PointsPlus value per serving: 4

    1   cup uncooked bulgur
    1   cup boiling water
    2   tablespoons olive oil
    2   tablespoons red wine vinegar
    2   tablespoons fresh lemon juice
    ½   teaspoon salt
    ¼   teaspoon freshly ground black pepper
    ½   cup diced seeded cucumber
    ½   cup diced seeded tomato
    2   tablespoons chopped green onions (about 1)
    1   (16-ounce) can chickpeas (garbanzo beans), rinsed and drained

1. Combine bulgur and 1 cup boiling water in a medium bowl. Cover and let stand 30 minutes.

2. While bulgur stands, combine oil and next 4 ingredients in a small bowl; stir well with a whisk.

3. Combine bulgur, oil mixture, cucumber, and remaining ingredients in a bowl; stir well. Cover and chill 2 hours. **Yield:** 6 servings (serving size: ¾ cup).

Per serving: CALORIES 170; FAT 5.5g (sat 0.7g, mono 1.9g, poly 0.4g); PROTEIN 5.5g; CARB 26.4g; FIBER 6.7g; CHOL 0mg; IRON 1.2mg; SODIUM 291mg; CALC 30mg

pictured on page 46

Arugula, Pear, and Gorgonzola Salad

prep: 8 minutes   *PointsPlus* value per serving: 2

    ½   cup refrigerated fat-free raspberry vinaigrette
    1   ounce crumbled Gorgonzola cheese (about ¼ cup)
    2   tablespoons chopped walnuts, toasted
    ½   teaspoon freshly ground black pepper
    2   Bartlett pears, cored and sliced
    1   (5-ounce) package baby arugula

1. Combine all ingredients in a large bowl; toss gently to coat. Serve immediately. **Yield:** 6 servings (serving size: 2 cups).

Per serving: CALORIES 88; FAT 3.2g (sat 1.2g, mono 0.2g, poly 1.2g); PROTEIN 2.2g; CARB 14.7g; FIBER 2.5g; CHOL 4mg; IRON 0.5mg; SODIUM 184mg; CALC 71mg

---

Menu
PointsPlus value per serving: 6

Lemony Bulgur Salad

½ whole-wheat pita round, warmed
PointsPlus value per serving: 2

Game Plan

1. Cook bulgur.

2. While bulgur stands:
   • Chop vegetables.
   • Rinse and drain chickpeas.
   • Whisk dressing together.
   • Warm pita.

3. Combine bulgur mixture.

Menu
PointsPlus value per serving: 6

Arugula, Pear, and Gorgonzola Salad

6 ounces grilled shrimp
PointsPlus value per serving: 4

Game Plan

1. While grill preheats:
   • Wash, core, and slice pears.
   • Chop and toast walnuts.

2. Grill shrimp.

3. Toss salad ingredients.

4. Serve shrimp with salad.

Menu
PointsPlus value
per serving: 8

Tex-Mex Layered Salad

1 ounce baked tortilla chips
PointsPlus value
per serving: 3

Game Plan

1. Shred lettuce.

2. Rinse and drain beans
and corn.

3. Assemble salad.

4. Process tomato mixture,
and top salad.

Tex-Mex Layered Salad

prep: 18 minutes

PointsPlus value per serving: 5

Layer the ingredients for the salad and blend the dressing before you leave for work. Pack them in separate containers, and refrigerate. When you get home, toss together the salad and dressing. Serve with multigrain chips or baked tortilla chips to add some crunch.

2   hearts of romaine lettuce, shredded (about 8½ cups)
2   (6-ounce) packages refrigerated grilled chicken breast strips
2   (2.25-ounce) cans sliced ripe olives, drained
1   (15-ounce) can black beans, rinsed and drained
1   (8.75-ounce) can whole-kernel corn, rinsed and drained
1   (2-ounce) jar diced pimiento, drained
4   ounces reduced-fat shredded cheddar cheese
     with jalapeño peppers (about 1 cup)
3   ounces tub-style light cream cheese (about ⅓ cup)
⅓   cup chopped green onions (about 2)
1   teaspoon ground cumin
1   (10-ounce) can diced tomatoes and green chiles, drained
1   (8-ounce) carton fat-free sour cream
1   garlic clove

1. Layer first 6 ingredients in a large bowl; top with cheddar cheese. Cover and chill until ready to serve.

2. Place cream cheese and next 5 ingredients in a blender or food processor; process until smooth. Toss dressing with salad just before serving. **Yield:** 8 servings (serving size: 1½ cups).

Per serving: CALORIES 191; FAT 6.1g (sat 2.6g, mono 0.6g, poly 0.1g); PROTEIN 18.2g; CARB 18.3g; FIBER 3.7g; CHOL 41mg; IRON 1.9mg; SODIUM 852mg; CALC 192mg

Salmon Pasta Salad with Lemon and Capers

prep: 17 minutes • **cook:** 10 minutes   *PointsPlus* value per serving: 8

Serve this salad for tonight's supper, and pack the remainder for tomorrow's lunch. Even when canned, salmon is a great source of omega-3 fatty acids, which help reduce the risk of heart disease.

8	ounces uncooked farfalle (bow tie pasta)
⅔	cup light mayonnaise
1½	teaspoons grated fresh lemon rind
1½	tablespoons fresh lemon juice
¼	teaspoon salt
¼	teaspoon freshly ground black pepper
⅓	cup chopped red onion
¼	cup chopped celery
2	tablespoons minced fresh parsley
1½	tablespoons capers, rinsed and drained
2	(6-ounce) cans skinless, boneless pink salmon in water, drained and shredded

1. Cook pasta according to package directions, omitting salt and fat. Rinse under cold water until cool; drain well.

2. Combine mayonnaise and next 4 ingredients in a large bowl. Add cooled pasta, onion, and remaining ingredients, and toss gently to combine. Cover and chill.

Yield: 6 servings (serving size: 1 cup).

Per serving: CALORIES 299; FAT 13.1g (sat 2.7g, mono 3.4g, poly 5.7g); PROTEIN 14.2g; CARB 31.6g; FIBER 1.6g; CHOL 38mg; IRON 1.6mg; SODIUM 553mg; CALC 88mg

---

Menu
PointsPlus value
per serving: 8

**Salmon Pasta Salad
with Lemon and Capers**

1 cup grapes
PointsPlus value
per serving: 0

Game Plan

1. Cook pasta.

2. While pasta cooks:
- Combine mayonnaise mixture.
- Chop onion, celery, and parsley.
- Rinse and drain capers.
- Drain and shred salmon.

3. Toss salad together.

Grilled Salmon Salade Niçoise

prep: 19 minutes • **cook:** 35 minutes • **other:** 10 minutes

PointsPlus value per serving: 9

Classic salade niçoise features tuna alongside potato, green beans, tomato, and olives. Here we've used heart-healthy salmon.

- 3 tablespoons stone-ground mustard
- 3 tablespoons white wine vinegar
- 2 tablespoons honey
- 4 teaspoons olive oil, divided
- ⅛ teaspoon salt
- 2 tablespoons fresh lemon juice
- 1 teaspoon kosher salt
- 1 teaspoon freshly ground black pepper
- 4 (6-ounce) salmon fillets
- 2 large eggs
- 1 pound small red potatoes, quartered
- ½ pound green beans, trimmed
- Cooking spray
- 4 cups fresh baby spinach
- ¼ cup niçoise or pitted kalamata olives, halved
- 1 large tomato, cut into wedges (about 2 cups)
- ½ red onion, thinly sliced

1. Combine mustard, vinegar, honey, 1 teaspoon oil, and ⅛ teaspoon salt in a small bowl; stir with a whisk. Set aside.

2. Combine 1 tablespoon olive oil, lemon juice, kosher salt, and pepper in a large zip-top plastic bag. Add fish to bag; seal. Marinate in refrigerator 10 minutes.

3. While fish marinates, place whole eggs and potato in a large saucepan or Dutch oven; cover with water. Bring to a boil. Reduce heat, and simmer 10 minutes. Remove eggs, and plunge into cold water; set aside. Cook potato 5 minutes; add green beans. Simmer 5 minutes or until vegetables are tender. Remove potato and beans, and plunge into cold water; drain. Peel eggs, and slice each into 6 wedges; set aside.

4. Preheat grill to medium-high heat.

5. Place fish, skin sides down, on grill rack coated with cooking spray, and grill, covered, 10 to 12 minutes or until fish flakes easily when tested with a fork or until desired degree of doneness. Remove skin from fish, and cut fish into chunks.

6. Combine spinach, olives, tomato, and onion in a large bowl; add vinegar mixture, potato, and beans, and toss to combine. Arrange salad on plates, and top with fish and eggs. **Yield:** 6 servings (serving size: 2 cups salad mixture, 3 ounces fish, and 2 egg wedges).

Per serving: CALORIES 353; FAT 15.2g (sat 3.2g, mono 7.8g, poly 3g); PROTEIN 29g; CARB 25.3g; FIBER 4.1g; CHOL 128mg; IRON 2.1mg; SODIUM 665mg; CALC 69mg

---

Menu

PointsPlus value per serving: 9

Grilled Salmon Salade Niçoise

1 cup blueberries
PointsPlus value per serving: 0

Game Plan

1. Marinate fish.

2. While potatoes and eggs cook:
- Preheat grill.
- Trim green beans.
- Slice salad vegetables.

3. Grill fish.

4. Assemble salad.

Tropical Shrimp Salad

prep: 30 minutes • **cook:** 7 minutes   *PointsPlus* value per serving: 7

**Sweet fruit complements the Caribbean spices on the shrimp.
If you're short on time, look for refrigerated precut pineapple
and mango.**

 2   tablespoons olive oil, divided
 1   tablespoon sherry vinegar
 ½   teaspoon honey mustard
 ½   teaspoon salt, divided
 ¼   teaspoon freshly ground black pepper
 2½ teaspoons salt-free Caribbean seasoning
 1½ pounds peeled and deveined medium shrimp
 1   cup chopped peeled mango
 1   cup coarsely chopped pineapple
 1   cup sliced green onions
 2   (8-ounce) packages mixed salad greens (about 8 cups)

1. Combine 1 tablespoon oil, vinegar, mustard, ¼ teaspoon salt, and pepper in a
small bowl, stirring with a whisk. Set aside.

2. Combine Caribbean seasoning, ¼ teaspoon salt, and shrimp in a large bowl;
toss well. Heat 1 tablespoon oil in a large nonstick skillet over medium-high heat.
Cook shrimp 3 to 4 minutes per side or until done.

3. Combine mango and next 3 ingredients in a bowl. Add dressing, tossing gently
to coat. Divide salad among 4 plates. Top with shrimp. **Yield:** 4 servings (serving
size: 2¼ cups salad mixture and about 7 shrimp).

Per serving: CALORIES 263; FAT 8.6g (sat 1.4g, mono 5.2g, poly 1.3g); PROTEIN 29.3g; CARB 17.6g; FIBER 4.8g; CHOL 252mg; IRON 5.7mg; SODIUM 626mg; CALC 142mg

---

Menu
PointsPlus value
per serving: 9

Tropical Shrimp Salad

**5 reduced-fat whole-grain
wheat crackers**
PointsPlus value
per serving: 2

Game Plan

1. Peel and devein shrimp.

2. While skillet heats:
 • Whisk dressing together.
 • Cut fruit and onions.
 • Season shrimp.

3. Cook shrimp.

4. Toss salad, and top
  with shrimp.

Menu

PointsPlus value
per serving: 10

Portobellos and
Flank Steak over Greens

1 whole-wheat dinner roll
PointsPlus value
per serving: 3

Game Plan

1. Marinate steak, mushrooms, and onion.

2. Grill steak and vegetables.

3. Slice steak, and cut mushrooms and onions.

4. Assemble salads, and drizzle with dressing.

Portobellos and Flank Steak over Greens

prep: 19 minutes • **cook:** 20 minutes • **other:** 2 hours and 35 minutes

PointsPlus value per serving: 7

Allowing the steak to stand before cutting it preserves the juices and makes for easier slicing. To enhance the steak's tenderness, cut the meat diagonally across the grain.

½ cup balsamic vinegar
⅓ cup olive oil
1 tablespoon Worcestershire sauce
½ teaspoon kosher salt
½ teaspoon freshly ground black pepper
2 garlic cloves, minced
1 (1½-pound) flank steak, trimmed
6 large portobello mushroom caps
1 large red onion, cut into ½-inch-thick slices
Cooking spray
6 cups mixed salad greens
1 cup cherry tomatoes, halved

1. Combine first 6 ingredients in a small bowl, stirring with a whisk until blended.
2. Combine steak, mushrooms, and onion in a large zip-top plastic bag. Add ½ cup vinegar mixture to bag; seal. Marinate in refrigerator 2½ hours, turning occasionally. Reserve remaining vinegar mixture.
3. Preheat grill to medium-high heat.
4. Remove steak and onion from bag, and place on grill rack coated with cooking spray. Grill 6 to 8 minutes on each side or until steak is desired degree of doneness and onion is tender. Remove mushrooms from bag; discard marinade. Place mushrooms on grill rack; grill 4 to 5 minutes on each side or until tender. Cut mushrooms into ½-inch-thick slices. Let steak stand 5 minutes. Cut steak diagonally across grain into thin slices.
5. Chop onion; combine onion and mushrooms in a medium bowl. Combine mixed greens and tomatoes, and arrange on plates. Top with mushroom mixture. Arrange steak over mushroom mixture; drizzle each serving with reserved vinegar mixture. Serve immediately. Yield: 6 servings (serving size: 1 cup salad, about ¾ cup mushroom mixture, 3 ounces steak, and 1 tablespoon dressing).

Per serving: CALORIES 283; FAT 13.6g (sat 3.4g, mono 7.2g, poly 1.3g); PROTEIN 28g; CARB 11.8g; FIBER 3.2g; CHOL 38mg; IRON 3.3mg; SODIUM 223mg; CALC 77mg

Orecchiette and Roasted Chicken Salad

prep: 5 minutes • **cook:** 14 minutes   *PointsPlus* value per serving: 7

2½   cups uncooked orecchiette ("little ears" pasta)
4   cups chopped spinach
2   cups chopped roasted chicken breast
⅓   cup light blue cheese dressing
2   ounces crumbled Maytag blue cheese (about ½ cup)
½   cup coarsely chopped walnuts, toasted (optional)

1. Cook pasta according to package directions, omitting salt and fat. While pasta cooks, combine spinach, chicken, and dressing in a large bowl. Toss with cooked pasta; top with crumbled blue cheese and, if desired, chopped walnuts. **Yield:** 6 servings (serving size: 1 cup salad and about 1 tablespoon blue cheese).

Per serving: CALORIES 265; FAT 5.4g (sat 2.5g, mono 1.2g, poly 0.5g); PROTEIN 22.5g; CARB 31g; FIBER 1.6g; CHOL 48mg; IRON 2.3mg; SODIUM 413mg; CALC 93mg

Menu
PointsPlus value
per serving: 7

**Orecchiette and Roasted
Chicken Salad**

1 cup halved strawberries
PointsPlus value
per serving: 0

Game Plan

1. Cook pasta.

2. While pasta cooks:
 • Chop spinach, chicken, and walnuts.
 • Slice strawberries.

3. Toss pasta ingredients together.

Italian Cobb Salad

prep: 8 minutes • **cook:** 4 minutes   *PointsPlus* value per serving: 6

Using prosciutto instead of ham puts an Italian spin on the traditional version of this famous salad.

Olive oil–flavored cooking spray
4   ounces thinly sliced prosciutto, chopped
1   (10-ounce) package Italian-blend salad greens
2   cups chopped cooked chicken breast
4   ounces preshredded part-skim mozzarella cheese (about 1 cup)
2   hard-cooked large eggs, sliced
½   cup fat-free balsamic vinaigrette

1. Heat a large nonstick skillet over medium-high heat; coat pan with cooking spray. Add prosciutto; sauté 4 minutes or until browned.
2. Arrange salad greens on 6 plates. Top with chicken, cheese, egg, and prosciutto. Drizzle with vinaigrette. **Yield:** 6 servings (serving size: about 1⅔ cups).

Per serving: CALORIES 231; FAT 10.7g (sat 4.5g, mono 3.8g, poly 1.4g); PROTEIN 25.5g; CARB 6.7g; FIBER 0.7g; CHOL 133mg; IRON 1.4mg; SODIUM 717mg; CALC 167mg

Menu
PointsPlus value
per serving: 10

Italian Cobb Salad

1 soft breadstick
PointsPlus value
per serving: 4

Game Plan

1. Hard-cook eggs.

2. While skillet heats:
 • Chop prosciutto and chicken.

3. Assemble salads on plates.

4. Warm breadsticks in oven.

Chef's Salad with Creamy Dijon Dressing

Menu
PointsPlus value per serving: 7

Chef's Salad with Creamy Dijon Dressing

5 rosemary flatbread crackers
PointsPlus value per serving: 2

Game Plan

1. Hard-cook eggs.

2. Chop chicken and eggs; dice ham.

3. Combine dressing.

4. Toss chicken mixture with dressing.

prep: 12 minutes

PointsPlus value per serving: 5

Drizzle our zesty homemade dressing over romaine lettuce topped with ham, chicken, eggs, and cheese for a hearty weeknight meal. Since the versatile dressing can easily be doubled, make extra to keep on hand to serve over a side salad later in the week. One tablespoon has a *PointsPlus* value of 1.

3   cups chopped cooked chicken breast
2   cups grape tomatoes
1   cup diced ham
2   ounces reduced-fat shredded sharp cheddar cheese (about ½ cup)
½   cup sliced ripe olives
2   hard-cooked large eggs, chopped
1   (10-ounce) package torn hearts of romaine lettuce
2   tablespoons light mayonnaise
2   tablespoons Dijon mustard
1   teaspoon sugar
1½ teaspoons cider vinegar
1   teaspoon bottled minced garlic
⅛   teaspoon salt
⅛   teaspoon freshly ground black pepper

1. Combine first 7 ingredients in a large bowl.

2. Stir together mayonnaise and next 6 ingredients until blended. Add dressing to chicken mixture; toss gently to coat. Serve immediately. **Yield:** 7 servings (serving size: 2 cups).

Per serving: CALORIES 212; FAT 8.5g (sat 2.7g, mono 2.8g, poly 1.7g); PROTEIN 27.2g; CARB 5.1g; FIBER 1.7g; CHOL 128mg; IRON 1.8mg; SODIUM 352mg; CALC 100mg

Main Dishes

Menu
PointsPlus value
per serving: 10

Pasta Primavera

1 cup baby spinach leaves
with cherry tomatoes
and 2 tablespoons light
balsamic vinaigrette
PointsPlus value
per serving: 1

Game Plan

1. While oven preheats:
• Cut vegetables.
• Thaw peas.

2. While vegetables roast:
• Cook pasta.
• Assemble salads.
• Shred cheese.

3. Toss pasta mixture.

Pasta Primavera

prep: 12 minutes • **cook:** 20 minutes   *PointsPlus* value per serving: 9

Roasting the carrots, squash, and garlic brings depth of flavor to this favorite springtime pasta dish.

2   medium carrots, cut into 1½-inch strips (1½ cups)
2   medium yellow squash, cut into 1½-inch strips (1½ cups)
3   garlic cloves, quartered
Cooking spray
8   ounces uncooked farfalle (bow tie pasta)
1   cup cherry tomatoes, halved
1   cup frozen petite green peas, thawed
⅓   cup whipping cream
1   ounce finely shredded fresh Parmesan cheese (about ¼ cup)
½   teaspoon salt
½   teaspoon freshly ground black pepper

1. Preheat oven to 500°.
2. Combine carrot, squash, and garlic on a jelly-roll pan coated with cooking spray; coat vegetables generously with cooking spray. Roast vegetables at 500° for 20 minutes or until tender and browned, stirring after 15 minutes.
3. While vegetables roast, cook pasta according to package directions, omitting salt and fat. Drain, reserving ¼ cup pasta water.
4. Place pasta in a large bowl. Stir in roasted vegetables, reserved pasta water, tomatoes, and remaining ingredients. Serve immediately. **Yield:** 4 servings (serving size: 1¾ cups).

Per serving: CALORIES 360; FAT 9.9g (sat 5.8g, mono 1.2g, poly 0.8g); PROTEIN 13.7g; CARB 56.3g; FIBER 6.1g;

31mg; IRON 3mg; SODIUM 435mg; CALC 128mg

Creamy Macaroni and Cheese

prep: 6 minutes • **cook:** 20 minutes   *PointsPlus* value per serving: 7

This comforting classic is surprisingly easy to make. Serve as an entrée with a green salad, or halve the serving size for a side dish with a *PointsPlus* value of 4.

    8   ounces uncooked elbow macaroni
    ¾   cup fat-free milk
    2   tablespoons all-purpose flour
    ¼   teaspoon salt
    5   ounces light processed cheese, cubed

1. Cook pasta according to package directions, omitting salt and fat. Drain.
2. While pasta cooks, combine milk, flour, and salt in a large saucepan, stirring with a whisk. Cook over medium heat 3 minutes or until thick, stirring constantly with whisk. Add cheese, stirring until cheese melts. Remove from heat.
3. Stir in pasta. Serve immediately. **Yield:** 4 servings (serving size: 1 cup).

Per serving: CALORIES 289; FAT 3.5g (sat 1.7g, mono 1g, poly 0.6g); PROTEIN 17.3g; CARB 45.7g; FIBER 1.9g; CHOL 13mg; IRON 2.3mg; SODIUM 673mg; CALC 310mg

Menu
PointsPlus value per serving: 9

Creamy Macaroni and Cheese

½ cup baby carrots
PointsPlus value per serving: 0

1 cup fat-free milk
PointsPlus value per serving: 2

Game Plan

1. While pasta cooks:
• Cube cheese.
• Prepare cheese sauce.

2. Combine pasta and cheese sauce.

3. Serve with carrots and milk.

Menu

PointsPlus value
per serving: 10

Cheese Ravioli Lasagna

1 cup steamed green beans
PointsPlus value
per serving: 0

Game Plan

1. While oven preheats:
   • Cook ravioli.

2. Assemble lasagna in pan.

3. While lasagna bakes:
   • Steam green beans.

Cheese Ravioli Lasagna

prep: 7 minutes • **cook:** 39 minutes • **other:** 10 minutes

PointsPlus value per serving: 10

Convenience products make this family-friendly dish easy to assemble, leaving you time to relax while it bakes.

2	(9-ounce) packages spinach and cheese ravioli
¾	cup matchstick-cut carrots
1½	cups chunky marinara sauce with mushrooms
	Cooking spray
1	cup part-skim ricotta cheese, divided
4	ounces preshredded part-skim mozzarella cheese, divided (about 1 cup)

1. Preheat oven to 350°.

2. Cook ravioli according to package directions, omitting salt and fat. After ravioli has cooked 3 minutes, add carrots; cook 1 minute. Drain. Combine ravioli mixture with marinara sauce in a medium bowl.

3. Layer one-third of pasta mixture in an 8 x 4–inch loaf pan coated with cooking spray; top with ⅓ cup ricotta cheese and ⅓ cup mozzarella cheese. Repeat layers twice.

4. Cover and bake at 350° for 35 minutes. Let stand 10 minutes before serving.

Yield: 6 servings (serving size: ⅙ casserole).

Per serving: CALORIES 365; FAT 12.9g (sat 7.4g, mono 1.1g, ploy 0.1g); PROTEIN 21.9g; CARB 41.5g; FIBER 2.1g; CHOL 52mg; IRON 2.4mg; SODIUM 783mg; CALC 379mg

pictured on page 113

Top-Shelf Veggie Pizza

prep: 16 minutes • **cook:** 21 minutes • **other:** 45 minutes

PointsPlus value per serving: 8

Look for fresh pizza dough in your supermarket's bakery, or purchase it from your local pizza parlor.

    1 pound refrigerated fresh pizza dough
    Olive oil–flavored cooking spray
    1 (1-ounce) package dried porcini mushrooms
    1 tablespoon olive oil, divided
    1 tablespoon yellow cornmeal
    1 garlic clove, minced
    1 red bell pepper, seeded and cut into thin strips
    1 (12-ounce) jar marinated quartered artichoke hearts, drained
    4 ounces preshredded part-skim mozzarella cheese (about 1 cup)
    ¼ cup chopped fresh basil (optional)

1. Place dough in a large bowl coated with cooking spray; turn to coat top. Cover and let rise in a warm place (85°), free from drafts, 45 minutes or until doubled in size. (Gently press two fingers into dough. If indentation remains, dough has risen enough.)

2. Preheat oven to 425°.

3. Rinse mushrooms with cold water; drain. Place mushrooms in water to cover in a saucepan. Bring to a boil, and cook 2 to 5 minutes. Drain mushrooms in a colander, discarding liquid. Chop mushrooms, and set aside.

4. Brush a 15-inch round pizza pan with 1 teaspoon oil; sprinkle with cornmeal. Roll dough into a 15-inch circle on a floured surface; place on prepared pan. Brush dough with 2 teaspoons oil, and sprinkle with garlic. Pierce surface liberally with a fork (do not allow dough to rise). Bake on bottom rack of oven at 425° for 15 minutes or until lightly browned.

5. While pizza dough bakes, heat a large nonstick skillet over medium-high heat; coat pan with cooking spray. Add bell pepper, and sauté 4 minutes. Add prepared mushrooms and artichokes; sauté 1 minute.

6. Top pizza crust with bell pepper mixture, leaving a ½-inch border, and sprinkle with cheese. Remove pizza from pizza pan, and place pizza directly on bottom rack of oven. Bake at 425° for 4 minutes or until cheese melts. Sprinkle with basil, if desired. **Yield:** 6 servings (serving size: 1 slice).

Per serving: CALORIES 324; FAT 9.4g (sat 3g, mono 1.7g, poly 0.3g); PROTEIN 14.2g; CARB 45g; FIBER 4.9g; CHOL 15mg; IRON 3.9mg; SODIUM 749mg; CALC 118mg

Menu
PointsPlus value per serving: 8

Top-Shelf Veggie Pizza

1 medium orange, cut into wedges
PointsPlus value per serving: 0

Game Plan

1. Allow dough to rise.

2. While oven preheats:
• Cook mushrooms.
• Roll out dough.

3. While dough bakes:
• Cook bell pepper.

4. Top pizza, and bake.

Parmesan Polenta Wedges with Ratatouille

prep: 25 minutes • **cook:** 32 minutes   *PointsPlus* value per serving: 8

Polenta is made from corn and is a delicious staple in Italian cuisine. This fat-free, cholesterol-free, high-fiber food helps bring the fiber content of this dish to 10 grams per serving, which is more than a third of the recommended daily intake.

 3 cups water
 1 cup quick-cooking polenta
 2.6 ounces grated fresh Parmesan cheese, divided (about ⅔ cup)
 ¾ teaspoon salt, divided
 Cooking spray
 1 (1-pound) eggplant, cut into ½-inch cubes
 1 large red bell pepper, seeded and cut into ½-inch cubes
 1 large zucchini, cut into ¾-inch cubes
 2 tablespoons minced fresh or 2 teaspoons dried thyme or rosemary
 1 tablespoon olive oil
 2 cups lower-sodium marinara sauce
 3 garlic cloves, minced

1. Bring 3 cups water to a boil in a heavy saucepan. Add polenta, stirring with a whisk; cook 2 to 3 minutes over medium-low heat or until mixture is slightly thick, stirring constantly. Stir in ⅓ cup Parmesan cheese and ¼ teaspoon salt. Spoon polenta into a pie plate coated with cooking spray. Cool.
2. Preheat oven to 450°.
3. Combine eggplant and next 4 ingredients in a large bowl, tossing to coat. Add ½ teaspoon salt.
4. Arrange vegetables in a single layer in a roasting pan coated with cooking spray. Bake at 450° for 20 minutes or until vegetables are tender.
5. Transfer vegetables to a Dutch oven; add marinara sauce and garlic. Bring to a simmer, and cook over medium heat 10 minutes.
6. Preheat broiler.
7. Sprinkle polenta with ⅓ cup cheese. Broil 3 minutes or until lightly browned. Serve polenta with ratatouille. **Yield:** 4 servings (serving size: 2 polenta wedges and 1 cup ratatouille).

Per serving: CALORIES 339; FAT 11.5g (sat 3.9g, mono 3.6g, poly 0.8g); PROTEIN 11.6g; CARB 40.3g; FIBER 10g; CHOL 12mg; IRON 0.8mg; SODIUM 894mg; CALC 169mg

Spanish Potato Tortilla

prep: 3 minutes • **cook:** 37 minutes   *PointsPlus* value per serving: 7

This Southwestern version of an Italian frittata is good served hot or at room temperature.

 3 cups thinly sliced peeled baking potato (about 1¼ pounds)
 1 tablespoon olive oil, divided
 1 cup thinly sliced onion
 ½ teaspoon salt, divided
 ½ teaspoon freshly ground black pepper, divided
 4 large eggs
 2 large egg whites
 ¼ teaspoon smoked paprika or regular paprika
 1 ounce grated fresh Parmesan cheese (about ¼ cup)
 2 tablespoons minced fresh parsley

1. Place potato in a large nonstick skillet. Add just enough water to cover (about 2½ cups). Bring to a boil over medium-high heat. Reduce heat; simmer 9 minutes, uncovered, just until potato is tender, stirring occasionally. Drain and transfer to a large bowl.

2. Heat 1 teaspoon oil in pan over medium heat. Add onion, ¼ teaspoon salt, and ¼ teaspoon pepper. Sauté 5 minutes or until lightly browned, stirring occasionally.

3. Combine eggs, egg whites, paprika, ¼ teaspoon salt, and ¼ teaspoon pepper in a large bowl, stirring with a whisk. Add potato and onion, stirring gently to combine.

4. Preheat oven to 350°.

5. Heat 2 teaspoons oil in a 10- to 11-inch ovenproof skillet over medium heat. Add potato mixture, smoothing into an even layer. Cook 1 minute without stirring. Bake at 350° for 20 minutes or until lightly browned and center is set. Remove from oven.

6. Preheat broiler.

7. Sprinkle tortilla with cheese. Broil 2 minutes or until cheese melts and is lightly browned. Invert tortilla onto a serving plate, and sprinkle with parsley.

Yield: 4 servings (serving size: 1 wedge).

Per serving: CALORIES 270; FAT 10g (sat 2.9g, mono 4.8, poly 1.2g); PROTEIN 13.1g; CARB 32.7g; FIBER 3.4g; CHOL 216mg; IRON 2.8mg; SODIUM 476mg; CALC 105mg

---

Menu
PointsPlus value
per serving: 7

Spanish Potato Tortilla

1 cup mixed berries
PointsPlus value
per serving: 0

Game Plan

1. Peel and slice potatoes.

2. While potatoes cook:
• Sauté onion mixture.
• Whisk together egg mixture.
• Preheat oven.

3. While tortilla bakes:
• Measure berries.

Menu
PointsPlus value
per serving: 12

Cornmeal-Crusted Catfish

½ cup deli coleslaw
PointsPlus value
per serving: 4

Game Plan

1. Combine cornmeal mixture.

2. Dredge fish fillets.

3. Cook fish.

4. Serve hot with tartar sauce and coleslaw.

Cornmeal-Crusted Catfish

prep: 12 minutes • **cook:** 20 minutes   *PointsPlus* value per serving: 8

The secret to a crispy crust is heating the skillet first and then cooking the fish over medium heat. Look for stone-ground cornmeal in specialty markets and health-food stores.

½ cup stone-ground yellow cornmeal
2 garlic cloves, minced
4 (6-ounce) catfish fillets
¼ cup fat-free milk
1 teaspoon Cajun seasoning
Cooking spray
2 teaspoons peanut or canola oil, divided
¼ cup fat-free tartar sauce

1. Combine cornmeal and garlic in a shallow dish.

2. Brush fillets with milk; sprinkle with seasoning. Dredge fillets in cornmeal mixture, pressing gently to coat.

3. Heat a large skillet over medium heat; coat pan with cooking spray. Add 1 teaspoon oil. Add 2 fillets to pan, and cook 5 to 6 minutes on each side or until fish flakes easily when tested with a fork or until desired degree of doneness. Remove fillets from pan; set aside, and keep warm.

4. Wipe drippings from pan with a paper towel. Repeat procedure with cooking spray, 1 teaspoon oil, and 2 fillets. Serve with tartar sauce. **Yield:** 4 servings (1 fillet and 1 tablespoon tartar sauce).

Per serving: CALORIES 331; FAT 15.5g (sat 3.5g, mono 7.1g, poly 3.4g); PROTEIN 28.3g; CARB 17.3g; FIBER 1g; CHOL 80mg; IRON 1.5mg; SODIUM 337mg; CALC 38mg

Spicy Orange-Glazed Salmon

prep: 11 minutes • **cook:** 8 minutes • **other:** 15 minutes

PointsPlus value per serving: 7

Spice up a weeknight meal with this sweet-hot, citrusy salmon dish. Using frozen, individually packaged salmon fillets is a great option for convenient dinners and saves you a last-minute stop at the fish market.

¼   cup chopped fresh cilantro
¼   cup thawed orange juice concentrate, undiluted
1   teaspoon olive oil
¼   teaspoon ground cumin
¼   teaspoon chili powder
¼   teaspoon salt
¼   teaspoon freshly ground black pepper
1   medium jalapeño pepper, seeded and minced
4   (6-ounce) salmon fillets (1¼ inches thick)
Cooking spray

1. Combine first 8 ingredients in a small bowl; stir well with a whisk.
2. Place fish in a shallow dish; pour orange juice mixture over fish, reserving 1 tablespoon orange juice mixture. Cover and marinate in refrigerator 15 minutes.
3. Preheat grill to medium-high heat.
4. Remove fish from marinade; discard marinade. Place fish, skin sides down, on grill rack coated with cooking spray; grill 4 to 5 minutes on each side or until fish flakes easily when tested with a fork or until desired degree of doneness. Remove fish from grill, and brush with reserved 1 tablespoon orange juice mixture. **Yield:** 4 servings (serving size: 1 fillet).

Per serving: CALORIES 287; FAT 14g (sat 3.2g, mono 6.3g, poly 3.3g); PROTEIN 36.4g; CARB 1.6g; FIBER 0.2g; CHOL 87mg; IRON 0.7mg; SODIUM 231mg; CALC 24mg

Menu
PointsPlus value per serving: 10

Spicy Orange-Glazed Salmon

½ cup steamed brown rice
PointsPlus value per serving: 3

1 cup steamed broccoli
PointsPlus value per serving: 0

Game Plan

1. While fish marinates:
  • Cook rice.
  • Steam broccoli.

2. Preheat grill.

3. Grill fish.

Menu

PointsPlus value
per serving: 6

Grouper Tacos
with Mango Salsa

1 cup pineapple cubes
PointsPlus value
per serving: 0

Game Plan

1. While grill preheats:
- Season fish.
- Chop salsa ingredients.
- Combine salsa
  ingredients.

2. While fish cooks:
- Warm tortillas.
- Cut pineapple.

3. Assemble tacos.

Grouper Tacos with Mango Salsa

prep: 25 minutes • **cook:** 14 minutes   *PointsPlus* value per serving: 6

Before assembling the tacos, toss 2 or 3 tablespoons of the juices that settle from the salsa with the angel hair slaw to moisten the slaw and distribute the flavors. One (24-ounce) jar of sliced mango will give you the 1½ cups needed for the salsa.

    4   (6-ounce) grouper fillets (about 1¼ to 1½ inches thick)
    6   tablespoons fresh lime juice, divided (about 4 limes)
    2   garlic cloves, minced
    ¾   teaspoon ground cumin, divided
    ½   teaspoon salt, divided
    ½   teaspoon freshly ground black pepper, divided
 1½   cups diced peeled mango
    ⅓   cup chopped red onion
    ¼   cup chopped fresh cilantro
 2½   tablespoons minced seeded jalapeño pepper (about 1 large)
    2   large garlic cloves, minced
        Cooking spray
   12   (5½-inch) corn tortillas
 1½   cups angel hair slaw

1. Preheat grill to medium-high heat.

2. Place fish in a shallow glass or ceramic baking dish; sprinkle with 2 tablespoons lime juice and 2 minced garlic cloves. Sprinkle with ½ teaspoon cumin, ¼ teaspoon salt, and ¼ teaspoon freshly ground black pepper. Set aside.

3. Combine diced mango, next 4 ingredients, ¼ cup lime juice, and ¼ teaspoon each of cumin, salt, and black pepper in a large bowl; toss well, and set aside.

4. Place fish on grill rack coated with cooking spray. Grill 7 to 8 minutes on each side or until fish flakes easily when tested with a fork or until desired degree of doneness. Flake fish into bite-sized pieces with fork.

5. Warm tortillas according to package directions.

6. Top each tortilla with about ¼ cup fish, 2 tablespoons mango salsa, and 2 tablespoons slaw. **Yield:** 6 servings (serving size: 2 tacos).

Per serving: CALORIES 228; FAT 2.4g (sat 0.3g, mono 0.6g, poly 1.0g); PROTEIN 24.7g; CARB 29.1g; FIBER 3.5g; CHOL 42mg; IRON 1.3mg; SODIUM 270mg; CALC 66mg

Seared Scallops with Herb Sauce

prep: 11 minutes • **cook:** 7 minutes   *PointsPlus* value per serving: 4

Remove the cast-iron skillet from the heat when preparing the sauce so you won't burn the herbs and create a bitter flavor.

1½	pounds large sea scallops (12 scallops)
¼	teaspoon kosher salt
¼	teaspoon freshly ground black pepper
2	teaspoons olive oil, divided
1	tablespoon chopped shallots
½	cup chardonnay or other dry white wine
1	tablespoon grated fresh lemon rind
1	tablespoon chopped fresh parsley
1	tablespoon chopped fresh chives
1	tablespoon chopped fresh basil

1. Pat scallops dry with paper towels; sprinkle with salt and pepper. Heat 1 teaspoon oil in a large cast-iron skillet over high heat. Add scallops to pan; cook 3 minutes on each side or until browned. Transfer scallops to a serving platter; keep warm.

2. Remove pan from heat, and add 1 teaspoon oil. Add shallots, and sauté 1 minute or until tender. Stir in wine and next 4 ingredients, scraping pan to loosen browned bits. Pour sauce over scallops, and serve immediately. **Yield:** 4 servings (serving size: 3 scallops and 1½ tablespoons sauce).

Per serving: CALORIES 175; FAT 3.7g (sat 0.5g, mono 1.7g, poly 0.8g); PROTEIN 28.8g; CARB 5.3g; FIBER 0.3g; CHOL 56mg; IRON 0.8mg; SODIUM 395mg; CALC 50mg

Menu
PointsPlus value per serving: 7

Seared Scallops with Herb Sauce

⅔ cup whole-wheat pasta
PointsPlus value per serving: 3

1 cup steamed sugar snap peas
PointsPlus value per serving: 0

Game Plan

1. Cook pasta.

2. While skillet heats:
- Pat scallops dry.
- Chop herbs, and grate rind.
- Steam peas.

3. Sauté scallops.

4. Serve scallops over pasta.

Menu

PointsPlus value
per serving: 9

Steamed Mussels
with Fennel and Tomatoes

1 ounce French bread, toasted
PointsPlus value
per serving: 2

1 cup mixed salad greens
and 2 tablespoons light
balsamic vinaigrette
PointsPlus value
per serving: 1

Game Plan

1. Cut vegetables.

2. Scrub and debeard mussels.

3. While mussels cook:
  • Toast bread.
  • Assemble salads.

Steamed Mussels with Fennel and Tomatoes

prep: 23 minutes • **cook:** 18 minutes   *PointsPlus* value per serving: 6

Serve with slices of crusty bread to soak up every drop of the savory broth.

4   teaspoons olive oil
1   cup finely chopped onion (about 1 small)
⅔   cup finely chopped fennel bulb (about ½ small bulb)
4   plum tomatoes, seeded and diced (about 1½ cups)
¼   teaspoon salt
¼   teaspoon freshly ground black pepper
3   garlic cloves, minced
1   cup dry white wine
3   pounds mussels, scrubbed and debearded
¼   cup finely chopped fresh parsley

1. Heat oil in a large Dutch oven over medium-high heat; add onion and fennel. Cook 5 minutes or until tender, stirring often. Add tomato and next 3 ingredients, and cook 3 minutes or until tomato softens, stirring often. Add wine, and bring to a boil. Add mussels; cover and simmer 10 minutes or until shells open. Remove from heat; discard any unopened shells. Place mussels in wide, shallow bowls; ladle broth over mussels. Sprinkle with parsley. **Yield:** 6 servings (serving size: about 15 mussels and ½ cup broth).

Per serving: CALORIES 256; FAT 8.4g (sat 1.4g, mono 3.4g, poly 1.9g); PROTEIN 28.2g; CARB 16.3g; FIBER 2g; CHOL 64mg; IRON 9.7mg; SODIUM 770mg; CALC 94mg

pictured on page 114

Grilled Shrimp Skewers with Lemon-Herb Feta

prep: 6 minutes • **cook:** 5 minutes • **other:** 45 minutes

PointsPlus value per serving: 4

These skewers are great served over hot couscous or orzo. Pair this dish with a side of steamed asparagus or zucchini. The lemon-herb feta would also be a delightful accompaniment to grilled fish. One serving or 4 teaspoons of feta has a *PointsPlus* value of 1.

Menu
PointsPlus value per serving: 7

Grilled Shrimp Skewers with Lemon-Herb Feta

½ cup cooked orzo
PointsPlus value per serving: 2

1 cup steamed zucchini
PointsPlus value per serving: 0

Game Plan

1. Soak skewers.

2. Thread shrimp on skewers.

3. While grill preheats:
  • Cook orzo.
  • Steam zucchini.

4. While shrimp cooks:
  • Combine feta mixture.

    8 (6-inch) wooden skewers
   24 medium shrimp (about 1 pound), peeled and deveined
    1 tablespoon olive oil, divided
    1 tablespoon chopped fresh oregano, divided
   ½ teaspoon grated fresh lemon rind
    2 tablespoons fresh lemon juice, divided
   ½ teaspoon freshly ground black pepper, divided
    1 garlic clove, minced
  Cooking spray
  1.3 ounces crumbled reduced-fat feta cheese (about ⅓ cup)

1. Soak wooden skewers in water 30 minutes.

2. Thread 3 shrimp onto each skewer, and place skewers in an 11 x 7–inch glass or ceramic baking dish.

3. Combine 1 teaspoon olive oil, 2 teaspoons oregano, lemon rind, 1 tablespoon lemon juice, ¼ teaspoon pepper, and garlic; pour over skewers, turning to coat. Cover and marinate in refrigerator 15 minutes.

4. Preheat grill to medium-high heat.

5. Remove skewers from dish; discard marinade. Place skewers on grill rack coated with cooking spray, and grill 5 to 6 minutes or until done, turning skewers occasionally.

6. Combine 2 teaspoons oil, 1 teaspoon oregano, 1 tablespoon lemon juice, ¼ teaspoon pepper, and feta cheese; toss gently.

7. Remove shrimp from grill, and place 2 skewers on each of 4 plates. Top with lemon-herb feta. **Yield:** 4 servings (serving size: 2 skewers and about 4 teaspoons feta).

Per serving: CALORIES 140; FAT 5.7g (sat 1.5g, mono 2.6g, poly 0.7g); PROTEIN 20.2g; CARB 1.6g; FIBER 0.3g; CHOL 171mg; IRON 2.7mg; SODIUM 327mg; CALC 68mg

Menu

PointsPlus value
per serving: 11

**Bacon-Cheeseburger
Meat Loaf**

**½ cup prepared
mashed potatoes**
PointsPlus value
per serving: 3

1 cup steamed green beans
PointsPlus value
per serving: 0

Game Plan

1. While oven preheats:
• Combine meat loaf
  ingredients.

2. While meat loaf cooks:
• Cook bacon.
• Combine ketchup and
  mustard.

3. While meat loaf stands:
• Steam green beans.
• Warm potatoes.

Bacon-Cheeseburger Meat Loaf

prep: 15 minutes • **cook:** 60 minutes • **other:** 10 minutes

PointsPlus value per serving: 8

⅓ cup ketchup
2 tablespoons prepared mustard
1 teaspoon Worcestershire sauce
½ teaspoon salt
½ teaspoon garlic powder
2 large egg whites
½ cup quick-cooking oats
1½ pounds ground round
  Cooking spray
1½ tablespoons ketchup
1 teaspoon prepared mustard
2 ounces reduced-fat shredded sharp cheddar cheese (about ½ cup)
3 slices center-cut bacon, cooked and crumbled

1. Preheat oven to 350°.
2. Combine first 6 ingredients in a large bowl, stirring with a whisk. Stir in oats. Crumble beef over oat mixture; stir just until blended.
3. Shape mixture into an 8 x 4–inch loaf; place on rack of a broiler pan coated with cooking spray.
4. Bake at 350° for 50 minutes.
5. Combine 1½ tablespoons ketchup and 1 teaspoon mustard; brush over loaf. Sprinkle with cheese and bacon. Bake an additional 10 minutes or until a thermometer registers 160°. Let stand 10 minutes; cut into 6 slices. **Yield:** 6 servings (serving size: 1 slice).

Per serving: CALORIES 303; FAT 15.9g (sat 6.5g, mono 5.1g, poly 0.6g); PROTEIN 28.7g; CARB 9.6g; FIBER 0.7g; CHOL 83mg; IRON 3mg; SODIUM 642mg; CALC 90mg

Quick Steak Fajitas

prep: 8 minutes • **cook:** 20 minutes   *PointsPlus* value per serving: 7

Searing the steak locks in its natural juices and cooks the beef quickly. Since these tortillas are packed full of beef and vegetables, try eating with a fork and knife.

1¼	pounds top sirloin steak, cut in half
1	teaspoon chili powder
1	teaspoon ground cumin
½	teaspoon salt, divided
1	tablespoon olive oil
1	medium-sized red or green bell pepper, seeded and thinly sliced
1	medium-sized yellow bell pepper, seeded and thinly sliced
1	large red onion, halved and thinly sliced
2	tablespoons fresh lime juice
5	(8-inch) low-fat whole-wheat flour tortillas

Cooking spray
Chopped tomato (optional)
Chopped cilantro (optional)
Reduced-fat sour cream (optional)
Lime wedges (optional)

1. Sprinkle steak with chili powder, cumin, and ¼ teaspoon salt.

2. Heat oil in a large nonstick skillet over medium-high heat. Add beef; cook 2 to 3 minutes on each side or until desired degree of doneness. Transfer to a serving plate; keep warm. Add bell pepper and onion to pan; cook 3 to 4 minutes over medium-high heat, stirring frequently. Remove from heat. Sprinkle with remaining ¼ teaspoon salt and lime juice.

3. Heat a small nonstick skillet over medium-high heat. Lightly coat both sides of each tortilla with cooking spray; cook each tortilla 1 minute on each side or until golden.

4. Cut steak diagonally across grain into thin slices. Toss steak with bell pepper mixture. Spoon beef and pepper mixture onto 1 side of each tortilla. Fold tortilla over mixture. If desired, top with tomato, cilantro, and sour cream, and garnish with lime wedges. **Yield:** 5 servings (serving size: 1 fajita).

Per serving: CALORIES 268; FAT 9.4g (sat 2.4g, mono 3.7g, poly 0.6g); PROTEIN 22.1g; CARB 25.6g; FIBER 5.8g; CHOL 45mg; IRON 1.7mg; SODIUM 612mg; CALC 33mg

---

Menu
PointsPlus value per serving: 7

Quick Steak Fajitas

1 cup grapes
PointsPlus value per serving: 0

Game Plan

1. Slice bell peppers and onion, and season steak.

2. Cook steak and vegetables.

3. Brown tortillas.

4. Assemble fajitas.

Menu

PointsPlus value
per serving: 11

Simple Dijon Flank Steak

½ cup brown rice
PointsPlus value
per serving: 3

Creamed Spinach (page 148)
PointsPlus value
per serving: 4

Game Plan

1. Marinate steak.

2. While broiler preheats:
  • Cook rice.
  • Sauté spinach.

3. While steak cooks:
  • Prepare cream sauce for spinach.

Simple Dijon Flank Steak

prep: 5 minutes • **cook:** 12 minutes • **other:** 24 hours and 5 minutes

PointsPlus value per serving: 4

Begin marinating this steak the evening before you plan to cook it. When you come home from work the next day, you can prepare this delicious steak in less than 20 minutes.

¼ cup Dijon mustard
¼ cup lower-sodium soy sauce
2 tablespoons fresh lime juice
1 teaspoon grated peeled fresh ginger
2 teaspoons sesame oil
2 garlic cloves
1 (1-pound) flank steak, trimmed (¾ inch thick)
Cooking spray

1. Combine first 6 ingredients in a large heavy-duty zip-top plastic bag; add steak. Seal bag; marinate in refrigerator 24 hours, turning bag occasionally.
2. Preheat broiler.
3. Remove steak from bag, discarding marinade. Place steak on a broiler pan coated with cooking spray. Broil 6 to 8 minutes on each side or until desired degree of doneness. Let steak stand 5 minutes. **Yield:** 4 servings (serving size: 3 ounces steak).

Per serving: CALORIES 169; FAT 6.8g (sat 2.4g, mono 2.4g, poly 0.5g); PROTEIN 24.7g; CARB 0.6g; FIBER 0g; CHOL 37mg; IRON 1.8mg; SODIUM 262mg; CALC 28mg

Soy-Lime Lamb Chops

prep: 7 minutes • **cook:** 8 minutes • **other:** 3 hours

PointsPlus value per serving: 5

¼ cup packed brown sugar
¼ cup lower-sodium soy sauce
1 tablespoon fresh lime juice
2 teaspoons white wine vinegar
½ teaspoon crushed red pepper
2 garlic cloves, pressed
8 (4-ounce) lamb loin chops, trimmed
Cooking spray

1. Combine first 6 ingredients in a large heavy-duty zip-top plastic bag. Add lamb; seal bag, and marinate in refrigerator 3 hours, turning occasionally.
2. Preheat grill to medium-high heat.
3. Remove lamb from bag, reserving marinade. Pour marinade into a 2-cup glass measure, and microwave at HIGH 1 minute or until boiling; cook 1 minute.
4. Place lamb on grill rack coated with cooking spray; grill 4 to 5 minutes on each side or until lamb is done, basting occasionally with reserved marinade. **Yield:** 4 servings (serving size: 2 lamb chops).

Per serving: CALORIES 212; FAT 7.3g (sat 2.6g, mono 2.9g, poly 0.7g); PROTEIN 26.2g; CARB 8.6g; FIBER 0.1g; CHOL 81mg; IRON 2.5mg; SODIUM 425mg; CALC 23mg

Menu
PointsPlus value
per serving: 9

Soy-Lime Lamb Chops

**Warm Fingerling
Potato Salad (page 83)**
PointsPlus value
per serving: 4

Game Plan

1. Marinate lamb chops.

2. Slice potatoes.

3. While potatoes cook:
• Preheat grill.
• Whisk dressing together.

4. Broil potatoes while chops
are on grill.

Game Plan

1. While grill preheats:
  • Season lamb chops.
  • Combine couscous
    ingredients, and cook.
  • Tear stems off spinach
    leaves.

2. Grill chops.

3. Sauté spinach until wilted.

Moroccan Lamb Chops with Couscous Pilaf

prep: 18 minutes • **cook:** 11 minutes • **other:** 5 minutes

PointsPlus value per serving: 10

Lamb is well suited for the North African flavors in this dish. For added flavor, stir golden raisins into the couscous pilaf.

  2 teaspoons Hungarian sweet paprika
1½ teaspoons ground cumin
  1 teaspoon garlic salt
  1 teaspoon ground coriander
  ½ teaspoon ground cinnamon
  8 (4-ounce) lamb loin chops, trimmed
  1 tablespoon olive oil
  ¾ cup fat-free, lower-sodium chicken broth
  ½ cup grated carrot
  ¼ cup orange juice
  ⅔ cup uncooked couscous
  ¼ cup minced green onions
  Cooking spray

1. Preheat grill to medium-high heat.
2. Combine paprika and next 4 ingredients in a small bowl; stir well to combine. Reserve 1½ teaspoons spice mixture, and set aside.
3. Brush lamb chops with olive oil; rub 4½ teaspoons spice mixture on both sides of lamb chops. Set lamb chops aside.
4. Combine chicken broth, carrot, orange juice, and reserved 1½ teaspoons spice mixture in a medium saucepan, and bring to a boil. Stir in couscous and green onions. Remove from heat; cover and let stand 5 minutes or until liquid is absorbed. Fluff mixture with a fork; keep warm.
5. Place lamb chops on grill rack coated with cooking spray. Grill 4 to 5 minutes on each side or until desired degree of doneness. Serve lamb chops with couscous. **Yield:** 4 servings (serving size: 2 lamb chops and ¾ cup couscous).

Per serving: CALORIES 385; FAT 14.2g (sat 4.9g, mono 7.2g, poly 1.6g); PROTEIN 35.9g; CARB 26.4g; FIBER 2.4g; CHOL 95mg; IRON 3.3mg; SODIUM 458mg; CALC 51mg

Top-Shelf Veggie Pizza | page 99

Grilled Shrimp Skewers with Lemon-Herb Feta | page 107

Rosemary-Garlic Pork Tenderloin | page 130

Ham Steak over Greens with Apple Cider Sauce | page 132

Shredded Brussels Sprouts with Pancetta and Walnuts | page 139

Grilled Okra | page 147

Orange-Sesame Snow Peas | page 144

Pesto-Vegetable
Medley | page 147

Risotto with Fresh Mozzarella, Tomatoes, and Basil | page 152

Parmesan-Basil Biscuits | page 159

Blueberry–Brown Sugar Muffins | page 161

123

Dark Chocolate Chunk Cookies | page 172

Blueberry-Walnut
Oatmeal Cookies | page 173

Lemon Drop Tartlets | page 174

Turtle Brownies | page 175

Caramel Apple
Galette | page 182

128

Veal with Mustard Cream Sauce

prep: 1 minute • **cook:** 12 minutes   *PointsPlus* value per serving: 4

Serve these tender veal cutlets topped with a tangy cream sauce alongside asparagus and rice or mashed potatoes.

  1 pound veal cutlets
  ½ teaspoon salt
  ½ teaspoon freshly ground black pepper
  2 teaspoons olive oil, divided
  ½ cup fat-free, lower-sodium chicken broth
  ⅔ cup fat-free half-and-half
  4 teaspoons Dijon mustard
  2 teaspoons fresh lemon juice
  ¼ cup chopped fresh parsley

1. Place veal between 2 sheets of plastic wrap; pound to ¼-inch thickness using a meat mallet or small heavy skillet. Sprinkle both sides of veal with salt and pepper.
2. Heat 1 teaspoon oil in a large nonstick skillet over medium-high heat. Add half of veal, and cook 1 minute on each side or until lightly browned. Remove veal from pan; keep warm. Repeat procedure with 1 teaspoon oil and remaining veal.
3. Add chicken broth to pan, scraping pan to loosen browned bits. Stir in half-and-half, mustard, and lemon juice. Reduce heat, and simmer 6 to 7 minutes or until sauce is slightly thick. Spoon sauce over veal, and sprinkle with chopped parsley.
Yield: 4 servings (serving size: about 3 ounces veal and 5 tablespoons sauce).

Per serving: CALORIES 172; FAT 4.4g (sat 0.9g, mono 2.3g, poly 0.5g); PROTEIN 24.7g; CARB 4.8g; FIBER 0.2g; CHOL 88mg; IRON 1.2mg; SODIUM 542mg; CALC 39mg

---

Menu
PointsPlus value
per serving: 10

Veal with Mustard Cream Sauce

½ cup yellow rice
PointsPlus value
per serving: 3

Marinated Asparagus (page 138)
PointsPlus value
per serving: 3

Game Plan

1. Steam, marinate, and chill asparagus.

2. Pound and season chops.

3. While rice cooks:
  • Heat skillet.
  • Chop parsley.

4. Cook chops and sauce.

pictured on page 115

Rosemary-Garlic Pork Tenderloin

prep: 20 minutes • **cook:** 23 minutes • **other:** 2 hours and 15 minutes

PointsPlus value per serving: 4

Fragrant rosemary and garlic enhance simple pork tenderloin. This herb paste also works well on chicken.

¼ cup minced fresh rosemary
¼ cup minced garlic (about 10 cloves)
1 tablespoon olive oil
2 teaspoons kosher salt
1 teaspoon freshly ground black pepper
2 (1-pound) pork tenderloins, trimmed
Cooking spray

1. Combine first 5 ingredients in a small bowl, mixing well to make a paste.
2. Make several 1-inch slits in pork, and stuff each slit with 1 teaspoon rosemary paste. Spread any remaining rosemary paste onto top and sides of pork. Cover and chill 2 hours.
3. Preheat grill to medium-high heat.
4. Place pork on grill rack coated with cooking spray. Grill pork 23 minutes or until a thermometer registers 155°, turning once. Remove pork from grill; cover and let stand 15 minutes. **Yield:** 8 servings (serving size: 3 ounces).

Note: While pork stands, its internal temperature will reach 160°.

Per serving: CALORIES 154; FAT 5.6g (sat 1.6g, mono 2.2g, poly 0.7g); PROTEIN 22.8g; CARB 1.8g; FIBER 0.3g; CHOL 63mg; IRON 1.4mg; SODIUM 516mg; CALC 17mg

---

Menu
PointsPlus value per serving: 7

Rosemary-Garlic Pork Tenderloin

½ cup prepared mashed potatoes
PointsPlus value per serving: 3

1 cup steamed broccoli
PointsPlus value per serving: 0

Game Plan

1. Chop rosemary and garlic.

2. Stuff pork with paste.

3. While pork grills:
   • Steam broccoli.
   • Warm potatoes.

Pork Medallions with Dried Cherries

prep: 5 minutes • **cook:** 19 minutes

PointsPlus value per serving: 6

Create a colorful plate by serving the pork and cherry sauce with wild rice and steamed sugar snap peas or carrots.

1   (1-pound) pork tenderloin, trimmed
2   teaspoons olive oil
Cooking spray
½   teaspoon salt
¼   teaspoon freshly ground black pepper
¼   teaspoon dried rubbed sage
¾   cup dry white wine, divided
½   cup finely chopped onion
½   cup fat-free, lower-sodium chicken broth
1   tablespoon apple jelly
1   teaspoon cornstarch
¼   teaspoon salt
⅛   teaspoon crushed red pepper
½   cup dried sweet cherries

1. Cut tenderloin crosswise into ¼-inch-thick slices. Heat oil in a large nonstick skillet coated with cooking spray over medium-high heat. Combine salt, black pepper, and sage, and sprinkle over both sides of pork medallions. Coat medallions with cooking spray. Add half of pork to pan; cook 3 minutes on each side or until browned. Remove pork from pan; keep warm. Repeat procedure with remaining pork.

2. Recoat pan with cooking spray. Add ¼ cup wine and onion; sauté 2 minutes. Combine ½ cup wine, broth, and next 4 ingredients in a small bowl, stirring until smooth. Add wine mixture and dried cherries to pan. Cook 4 minutes or until thick, stirring constantly. Spoon cherry mixture over pork. **Yield:** 4 servings (serving size: 3 ounces pork and 2½ tablespoons sauce).

Per serving: CALORIES 255; FAT 6.2g (sat 1.7g, mono 2.6g, poly 0.8g); PROTEIN 25g; CARB 22.3g; FIBER 2.4g; CHOL 74mg; IRON 2mg; SODIUM 571mg; CALC 35mg

---

Menu

PointsPlus value per serving: 8

Pork Medallions with Dried Cherries

½ **cup wild rice**
PointsPlus value per serving: 2

1 **cup steamed carrots**
PointsPlus value per serving: 0

Game Plan

1. Trim and slice pork.

2. While skillet heats:
 • Cook rice.
 • Steam carrots.

3. Brown pork.

4. Prepare cherry sauce.

pictured on page 116

Ham Steak over Greens with Apple Cider Sauce

prep: 5 minutes • **cook:** 23 minutes *PointsPlus* value per serving: 7

Look for bags of prewashed chopped mustard greens in your grocer's produce section. The sweetness of apple cider complements the peppery flavor of the mustard greens.

1 pound lean ham steak, trimmed
1 tablespoon plus 1 teaspoon butter, divided
½ cup chopped onion
3 garlic cloves, minced
1 (16-ounce) package chopped mustard greens
1½ cups apple cider, divided
½ teaspoon salt
¼ teaspoon freshly ground black pepper

1. Heat a large nonstick skillet over medium-high heat; add ham steak. Cook 3 minutes on each side or until browned. Remove from pan, and keep warm.
2. Melt 1 tablespoon butter in pan over medium-high heat. Add onion and garlic; sauté 3 minutes. Add half of mustard greens; cover and cook 2 minutes or until slightly wilted. Add remaining greens and ½ cup cider. Cover and cook 15 minutes, stirring occasionally. Stir in salt and pepper.
3. While greens cook, bring 1 cup cider to a boil in a small saucepan. Cook 10 minutes or until reduced to ¼ cup. Remove from heat, and stir in 1 teaspoon butter.
4. Divide wilted greens among 4 plates. Divide ham steak evenly over greens. Drizzle cider sauce over ham and greens. **Yield:** 4 servings (serving size: 3 ounces ham, about ¾ cup mustard greens, and 1 tablespoon sauce).

Per serving: CALORIES 283; FAT 9.9g (sat 4.5g, mono 3.8g, poly 0.8g); PROTEIN 27.9g; CARB 21.5g; FIBER 4.1g; CHOL 79mg; IRON 2.8mg; SODIUM 425mg; CALC 134mg

Menu
PointsPlus value per serving: 11

Ham Steak over Greens with Apple Cider Sauce

½ cup prepared mashed sweet potatoes
PointsPlus value per serving: 4

Game Plan

1. While skillet heats:
• Trim ham.
• Chop onion, and mince garlic.
2. Brown ham.
3. Sauté greens, and make sauce.
4. Warm sweet potatoes.

Herbed Chicken Sticks

prep: 26 minutes • **cook:** 20 minutes   *PointsPlus* value per serving: 8

Panko breadcrumbs, found in the Asian-foods section of your super-market, provide the crunchy coating in this family favorite. Serve the chicken sticks solo, atop a main-dish salad, or tucked in a wrap.

1¾   cups panko (Japanese breadcrumbs)
 2   tablespoons minced fresh parsley
1½   tablespoons minced fresh thyme
1½   tablespoons minced fresh rosemary
 ¾   cup low-fat buttermilk
1½   pounds skinless, boneless chicken breast, cut into ½-inch strips
 ¼   teaspoon salt
 ¼   teaspoon pepper
 2   tablespoons butter, melted

1. Preheat oven to 425°.
2. Combine first 4 ingredients in a shallow bowl, stirring well. Place buttermilk in another shallow bowl.
3. Dip chicken strips in buttermilk, and dredge in panko mixture. Place breaded chicken on a baking sheet lined with parchment paper; sprinkle with salt and pepper. Drizzle melted butter over chicken. Bake at 425° for 20 minutes or until lightly browned, turning after 10 minutes. **Yield:** 4 servings (serving size: about 5 chicken tenders).

Per serving: CALORIES 348; FAT 8.6g (sat 4.1g, mono 1.9g, poly 0.7g); PROTEIN 44.3g; CARB 20.3g; FIBER 1.8g; CHOL 114mg; IRON 2.2mg; SODIUM 407mg; CALC 86mg

Menu
PointsPlus value
per serving: 10

Herbed Chicken Sticks

1 cup romaine lettuce
with cherry tomatoes
and 2 tablespoons fat-free
ranch dressing
PointsPlus value
per serving: 2

Game Plan

1. While oven preheats:
 • Combine breadcrumb
   mixture.
 • Cut chicken into strips.
 • Dredge chicken.

2. Cook chicken.

3. Prepare salad.

Menu
PointsPlus value
per serving: 11

Baked Chicken
and Risotto Casserole

1 cup steamed green beans
PointsPlus value
per serving: 0

Game Plan

1. Skin and season chicken.

2. Brown chicken.

3. Combine casserole
ingredients.

4. While casserole bakes:
• Steam green beans.
• Grate cheese.

Baked Chicken and Risotto Casserole

prep: 9 minutes • **cook:** 43 minutes • **other:** 5 minutes

PointsPlus value per serving: 11

This recipe has the goodness of a traditional Italian risotto without all the stirring, since it bakes in the oven.

4 (8-ounce) bone-in chicken breast halves, skinned
½ teaspoon salt
½ teaspoon freshly ground black pepper
1 tablespoon olive oil
2 cups minced onion (about 2 large)
½ cup dry white wine
1 (14-ounce) can fat-free, lower-sodium chicken broth
1 bay leaf
1 cup uncooked Arborio rice
1 ounce grated fresh Parmesan cheese (about ¼ cup)
Chopped fresh flat-leaf parsley (optional)

1. Preheat oven to 350°.

2. Sprinkle chicken with salt and pepper. Heat oil in an ovenproof Dutch oven over medium-high heat. Add chicken; cook 3 to 4 minutes on each side or until browned. Remove chicken, reserving drippings in pan.

3. Add onion; cook 4 minutes. Add wine, scraping pan to loosen browned bits. Add broth and bay leaf; bring to a boil. Stir in rice, and arrange chicken, rib sides down, in pan. Cover and bake at 350° for 30 minutes or until chicken is done. Remove from oven, and let stand, covered, 5 minutes. Discard bay leaf. Sprinkle with cheese and, if desired, parsley. **Yield:** 4 servings (serving size: 1 chicken breast half and 1 cup rice).

Per serving: CALORIES 425; FAT 7.2g (sat 1.9g, mono 3.4g, poly 0.8g); PROTEIN 42.4g; CARB 46.7g; FIBER 3.4g; CHOL 89mg; IRON 1.6mg; SODIUM 763mg; CALC 101mg

Slow-Cooker Chicken and Sausage Paella

prep: 8 minutes • **cook:** 4 hours and 40 minutes

PointsPlus value per serving: 9

    2   cups frozen chopped onion
    1¾ cups uncooked converted rice
    2   tablespoons bottled minced garlic
    1   teaspoon dried thyme
    1   teaspoon freshly ground black pepper
    1   (14½-ounce) can Italian-style stewed tomatoes, undrained and chopped
    1   (9-ounce) package frozen chopped cooked chicken
    ½   (14-ounce) package low-fat smoked sausage, sliced
    Cooking spray
    1¾ cups water
    ½   teaspoon saffron threads
    1   (14-ounce) can fat-free, lower-sodium chicken broth
    1   cup frozen petite green peas

1. Place first 8 ingredients in a 4-quart electric slow cooker coated with cooking spray. Combine 1¾ cups water, saffron, and broth; add to cooker. Stir well. Cover and cook on LOW 4 hours and 30 minutes.

2. Remove lid; quickly stir in peas. Cover and cook on HIGH 10 minutes.

Yield: 6 servings (serving size: about 1¾ cups).

Per serving: CALORIES 362; FAT 2.1g (sat 0.7g, mono 0.9g, poly 0.4g); PROTEIN 21.2g; CARB 63.9g; FIBER 3.9g; CHOL 30mg; IRON 3.4mg; SODIUM 852mg; CALC 57mg

Menu
PointsPlus value per serving: 9

Slow-Cooker Chicken and Sausage Paella

1 orange, cut into wedges *PointsPlus* value per serving: 0

Game Plan

1. Chop tomatoes, and slice sausage.

2. Combine paella ingredients in slow cooker, and cook.

3. Add peas.

4. Slice oranges.

Menu

PointsPlus value
per serving: 11

Curried Chicken Thighs

½ cup prepared couscous
PointsPlus value
per serving: 3

Game Plan

1. Marinate chicken.

2. Preheat grill.

3. While chicken cooks:
• Cook couscous.

4. Serve onions and chicken
over couscous.

Curried Chicken Thighs

prep: 20 minutes • **cook:** 12 minutes • **other:** 8 hours

PointsPlus value per serving: 8

Aromatic and distinctively flavorful, curry powder and fresh ginger add a warm, spicy note to the sweet yogurt mixture that's used to marinate the chicken. Couscous or basmati rice is an ideal accompaniment for the grilled chicken and onions.

    ½   cup plain low-fat yogurt
    2   tablespoons honey
    2   teaspoons curry powder
    1   teaspoon grated peeled fresh ginger
    1   garlic clove, minced
    8   (3-ounce) skinless, boneless chicken thighs
    ¾   teaspoon salt
    1   red onion, cut into ¼-inch-thick slices
    Cooking spray
    2   tablespoons minced fresh cilantro
    4   teaspoons fresh lemon juice
    2   teaspoons canola oil

1. Combine first 5 ingredients in a medium bowl, stirring with a whisk. Pour into a large heavy-duty zip-top plastic bag; add chicken. Seal bag, and marinate in refrigerator 8 hours, turning bag occasionally.

2. Preheat grill to medium-high heat.

3. Remove chicken from bag, discarding marinade. Sprinkle chicken with salt, and coat chicken and onion with cooking spray. Place on grill rack coated with cooking spray; cook 6 minutes on each side or until chicken is done. Remove chicken and onion from grill; cut onion slices in half, and separate into strips.

4. Combine cilantro, lemon juice, and oil in a medium bowl. Add onion strips; toss well. Spoon onion mixture onto a serving platter. Top with chicken. **Yield:** 4 servings (serving size: 2 chicken thighs and ⅓ cup onion mixture).

Per serving: CALORIES 319; FAT 15.5g (sat 3.9g, mono 6.4g, poly 3.6g); PROTEIN 31.8g; CARB 12g; FIBER 0.7g; CHOL 113mg; IRON 1.9mg; SODIUM 559mg; CALC 54mg

Side Dishes

Grocery List

- ☐ 1½ pounds asparagus
- ☐ White wine vinegar
- ☐ 1 bunch parsley
- ☐ 1 bunch green onions
- ☐ 1 (1-ounce) jar Italian seasoning
- ☐ 1 (2-ounce) jar diced pimiento
- ☐ Check staples: olive oil, garlic, sugar, salt, pepper

Marinated Asparagus

prep: 7 minutes • **cook:** 3 minutes • **other:** 8 hours

PointsPlus value per serving: 3

This is a fantastic make-ahead dish that only gets better the longer it marinates.

8	cups water
1½	pounds asparagus, trimmed
¼	cup olive oil
¼	cup white wine vinegar
3	tablespoons chopped fresh parsley
3	tablespoons finely chopped green onions
3	garlic cloves, minced
1	teaspoon sugar
1	teaspoon Italian seasoning
¼	teaspoon salt
¼	teaspoon freshly ground black pepper
1	(2-ounce) jar diced pimiento, undrained

1. Bring 8 cups water to a boil in a Dutch oven; add asparagus, and cook 3 to 4 minutes or until crisp-tender. Remove asparagus with a slotted spoon. Plunge into ice water; drain. Pat asparagus dry with paper towels. Place in a large zip-top plastic bag.

2. Combine oil and next 9 ingredients in a small bowl, stirring with a whisk. Pour marinade over asparagus in bag. Seal bag, and refrigerate 8 hours.

3. Transfer asparagus to a serving dish; drizzle marinade over asparagus.

Yield: 6 servings (serving size: about 10 spears).

Per serving: CALORIES 102; FAT 9.5g (sat 1.4g, mono 6.7g, poly 1.4g); PROTEIN 1.7g; CARB 4.6g; FIBER 1.7g; CHOL 0mg; IRON 1.7mg; SODIUM 102mg; CALC 27mg

pictured on page 117

Shredded Brussels Sprouts with Pancetta and Walnuts

prep: 9 minutes • **cook:** 11 minutes

PointsPlus value per serving: 3

- 1 tablespoon brown sugar
- 2 tablespoons cider vinegar
- 2 ounces thinly sliced pancetta
- 1 pound Brussels sprouts, trimmed and thinly sliced
- 2 tablespoons chopped walnuts, toasted
- ¼ teaspoon freshly ground black pepper

1. Combine brown sugar and vinegar in a small bowl.

2. Cook pancetta in a large nonstick skillet over medium heat until crisp. Remove pancetta from pan, reserving drippings in pan; drain pancetta on paper towels, and crumble. Add Brussels sprouts to hot drippings in pan; sauté 4 minutes or until crisp-tender. Remove from heat; drizzle Brussels sprouts immediately with vinegar mixture, scraping pan to loosen browned bits. Spoon mixture into a bowl; add crumbled pancetta, nuts, and pepper, tossing well. **Yield:** 6 servings (serving size: ½ cup).

Per serving: CALORIES 97; FAT 5g (sat 1.8g, mono 1.5g, poly 1.5g); PROTEIN 6.1g; CARB 9.4g; FIBER 3.1g; CHOL 12mg; IRON 1.2mg; SODIUM 232mg; CALC 36mg

> **Grocery List**
> - ☐ Cider vinegar
> - ☐ 2 ounces pancetta
> - ☐ 1 pound Brussels sprouts
> - ☐ 1 (2-ounce) bag chopped walnuts
> - ☐ Check staples: brown sugar, pepper

Broccoli with Garlic-Herb Butter

prep: 4 minutes • **cook:** 4 minutes

PointsPlus value per serving: 1

- 2 tablespoons light stick butter
- 2 tablespoons chopped fresh parsley
- 2 garlic cloves, minced
- 4 cups broccoli florets
- 2 tablespoons water
- ¼ teaspoon salt
- ¼ teaspoon freshly ground black pepper

1. Place butter in a small microwave-safe dish. Microwave at HIGH 15 seconds or until melted. Stir in parsley and garlic.

2. Place broccoli florets in a large microwave-safe bowl. Add 2 tablespoons water, and cover with wax paper. Microwave at HIGH 4 minutes or until crisp-tender. Drain well. Add butter mixture, salt, and pepper; toss gently to coat. **Yield:** 4 servings (serving size: 1 cup).

Per serving: CALORIES 48; FAT 3.3g (sat 1.8g, mono 0g, poly 0.1g); PROTEIN 2.3g; CARB 4.9g; FIBER 2.2g; CHOL 8mg; IRON 0.8mg; SODIUM 213mg; CALC 40mg

> **Grocery List**
> - ☐ 1 box light stick butter
> - ☐ 1 bunch parsley
> - ☐ 1 (12-ounce) bag broccoli florets
> - ☐ Check staples: garlic, salt, pepper

Spicy Asian Cabbage

prep: 12 minutes • **cook:** 6 minutes   *PointsPlus* value per serving: 2

Grocery List

☐ Sesame oil
☐ 1 head cabbage
☐ 1 red bell pepper
☐ 2 bunches green onions
☐ 1 (10-ounce) bag matchstick-cut carrots
☐ 1 small piece fresh ginger
☐ 1 small jar jalapeño jelly
☐ Lower-sodium soy sauce
☐ Check staple: cooking spray

  2 teaspoons dark sesame oil
Cooking spray
  4 cups shredded green cabbage
  1 cup thinly sliced red bell pepper
  1 cup thinly sliced green onions
  ½ cup matchstick-cut carrots
  2 teaspoons grated peeled fresh ginger
  3 tablespoons hot jalapeño jelly
  2 tablespoons lower-sodium soy sauce

1. Heat oil in a large nonstick skillet coated with cooking spray over medium-high heat. Add cabbage and next 4 ingredients; sauté 4 minutes or until vegetables are crisp-tender. Add jelly and soy sauce; cook 1 minute or until jelly melts. Stir to coat. **Yield:** 5 servings (serving size: ½ cup).

Per serving: CALORIES 76; FAT 2g (sat 0.3g, mono 0.8g, poly 0.8g); PROTEIN 1.4g; CARB 13.6g; FIBER 2.9g; CHOL 0mg; IRON 0.7mg; SODIUM 284mg; CALC 43mg

Maple-Roasted Carrots and Parsnips

prep: 16 minutes • **cook:** 45 minutes   *PointsPlus* value per serving: 5

Grocery List

☐ Maple syrup
☐ 1 pound carrots
☐ 1 pound parsnips
☐ Balsamic vinegar
☐ Check staples: olive oil, salt, pepper

For the best browning, spread the carrots and parsnips in a single layer, and stir only once during roasting.

  2 tablespoons maple syrup
1½ tablespoons olive oil
  ¼ teaspoon salt
  ¼ teaspoon freshly ground black pepper
  1 pound carrots, cut into 1¼-inch sticks (about 3 cups)
  1 pound parsnips, cut into 1¼-inch sticks (about 3 cups)
  1 tablespoon balsamic vinegar

1. Preheat oven to 425°.
2. Combine first 6 ingredients in a large bowl; toss to coat. Arrange vegetable mixture in a single layer on a foil-lined jelly-roll pan. Bake at 425° for 45 minutes or until browned and crisp, turning once. Drizzle with vinegar, and serve immediately. **Yield:** 5 servings (serving size: ⅔ cup).

Per serving: CALORIES 165; FAT 4.7g (sat 0.6g, mono 3g, poly 0.7g); PROTEIN 2g; CARB 31g; FIBER 4.4g; CHOL 0mg; IRON 0.9mg; SODIUM 191mg; CALC 69mg

Roasted Root Vegetables

prep: 13 minutes • **cook:** 25 minutes   *PointsPlus* value per serving: 3

To store beets and carrots, trim the stems to about 1 inch and keep the roots in plastic bags in the refrigerator about two weeks. Peel the beets under cold running water to prevent them from staining your fingers.

½   pound beets (about 3 medium), trimmed and peeled
3   medium carrots, peeled
1   medium onion
1   tablespoon extra-virgin olive oil
2   teaspoons balsamic vinegar
1   teaspoon sugar
⅛   teaspoon salt
⅛   teaspoon crushed red pepper

1. Preheat oven to 450°.
2. Line a large baking sheet with foil.
3. Cut beets into 8 wedges each. Cut carrots in half lengthwise, and cut halves into 3-inch pieces. Remove skin from onion; cut into large wedges, leaving root intact.
4. Place beets, carrot, and onion in a medium bowl; drizzle with oil, and toss well. Arrange vegetables in a single layer on prepared pan. Bake at 450° for 15 minutes; stir and bake an additional 10 minutes or until tender.
5. Return vegetables to bowl; add vinegar and remaining ingredients. Toss gently to coat. **Yield:** 4 servings (serving size: ½ cup).

Per serving: CALORIES 93; FAT 3.7g (sat 0.5g, mono 0.8g, poly 0.3g); PROTEIN 1.6g; CARB 14.7g; FIBER 2.2g; CHOL 0mg; IRON 0.8mg; SODIUM 150mg; CALC 31mg

Grocery List
☐ ½ pound beets
☐ 1 small bag carrots
☐ 1 onion
☐ Balsamic vinegar
☐ 1 (1-ounce) jar crushed red pepper
☐ Check staples: olive oil, sugar, salt

Cauliflower with Green Onions

prep: 6 minutes • **cook:** 4 minutes   *PointsPlus* value per serving: 1

If the florets in the package are large, cut them into bite-sized pieces using a sharp paring knife. The smaller pieces will steam faster.

1 (10 ⅜-ounce) package cauliflower florets (about 3½ cups)
3 tablespoons thinly sliced green onions
2 tablespoons grated Parmesan cheese
2 teaspoons butter
¼ teaspoon kosher salt
⅛ teaspoon coarsely ground black pepper

1. Steam cauliflower, covered, 4 minutes or until tender.
2. Transfer cauliflower to a medium bowl; add green onions and remaining ingredients. Toss well to combine. **Yield:** 4 servings (serving size: ¾ cup).

Per serving: CALORIES 48; FAT 2.7g (sat 1.7g, mono 0.7g, poly 0.1g); PROTEIN 2.5g; CARB 4.4g; FIBER 2g; CHOL 7mg; IRON 0.4mg; SODIUM 192mg; CALC 48mg

Sherry-Creamed Mushrooms

prep: 10 minutes • **cook:** 15 minutes   *PointsPlus* value per serving: 2

Cooking spray
½ cup finely chopped onion
1 garlic clove, minced
¼ cup dry sherry
1 teaspoon olive oil
¼ teaspoon salt
1 pound small mushrooms
¼ cup reduced-fat sour cream
⅛ teaspoon freshly ground black pepper
2 tablespoons chopped fresh parsley

1. Heat a large nonstick skillet over medium-high heat; coat pan with cooking spray. Add chopped onion, and sauté 2 minutes or until onion begins to brown. Add garlic, and sauté 15 seconds or until lightly browned. Add sherry and next 3 ingredients. Cover, reduce heat to medium, and cook 8 minutes or until tender. Uncover and cook 4 minutes or until liquid thickens. Remove from heat, and stir in sour cream and pepper. Sprinkle with chopped parsley. **Yield:** 5 servings (serving size: ½ cup).

Per serving: CALORIES 56; FAT 2.7g (sat 1.1g, mono 1.1g, poly 0.3g); PROTEIN 3.4g; CARB 5.4g; FIBER 1.3g; CHOL 5mg; IRON 0.6mg; SODIUM 130mg; CALC 23mg

Sautéed Green Beans with Bacon

prep: 7 minutes • **cook:** 18 minutes   *PointsPlus* value per serving: 2

2   pounds green beans, trimmed
4   bacon slices, chopped
1   cup chopped onion
½   cup chopped green bell pepper
½   teaspoon salt
½   teaspoon freshly ground black pepper

1. Cook green beans in boiling water 12 minutes or until tender. Drain.
2. While green beans cook, place bacon in a large nonstick skillet, and cook over medium heat 7 minutes or until crisp. Remove bacon from pan, reserving 1 tablespoon drippings in pan; set bacon aside.
3. Add onion and bell pepper to drippings in pan; sauté 4 minutes or until tender. Stir in green beans, salt, and pepper; sauté 2 to 3 minutes or until thoroughly heated. Stir in bacon. **Yield:** 6 servings (serving size: ⅔ cup).

Per serving: CALORIES 97; FAT 4.1g (sat 1.5g, mono 1.8g, poly 0.5g); PROTEIN 4.4g; CARB 12.7g; FIBER 5.2g; CHOL 7mg; IRON 1.6mg; SODIUM 307mg; CALC 58mg

Grocery List

☐ 2 pounds green beans
☐ 1 (12-ounce) package bacon
☐ 1 onion
☐ 1 green bell pepper
☐ Check staples: salt, pepper

Grilled Chipotle-Lime Corn

prep: 10 minutes • **cook:** 10 minutes   *PointsPlus* value per serving: 3

The spicy and smoky flavors of the chipotle seasoning helped this recipe score our Test Kitchen's highest rating.

1   teaspoon salt-free Southwest chipotle seasoning
1   teaspoon grated fresh lime rind
¼   teaspoon salt
1½ tablespoons fresh lime juice
4   medium ears corn

1. Preheat grill to medium-high heat.
2. Combine first 4 ingredients in a small bowl. Place corn on a large plate; brush with lime mixture, reserving drippings on plate.
3. Grill corn 10 minutes, turning once or until corn is slightly charred and done. Return corn to plate, and brush with reserved drippings. **Yield:** 4 servings (serving size: 1 ear of corn).

Per serving: CALORIES 79; FAT 1.7g (sat 0.3g, mono 0.3g, poly 0.5g); PROTEIN 3.9g; CARB 17.7g; FIBER 2.5g; CHOL 0mg; IRON 0.5mg; SODIUM 159mg; CALC 3mg

Grocery List

☐ 1 (2.5-ounce) jar salt-free Southwest chipotle seasoning
☐ 1 lime
☐ 4 ears corn
☐ Check staple: salt

pictured on page 119

Orange-Sesame Snow Peas

prep: 8 minutes • **cook:** 3 minutes   *PointsPlus* value per serving: 2

Snow peas are best and will keep their fresh crunch when you cook them just enough to bring out the bright green color.

Grocery List

☐ 1 (12-ounce) can frozen orange juice concentrate
☐ Lower-sodium soy sauce
☐ 1 (1-ounce) jar toasted sesame seeds
☐ 1 small orange
☐ Sesame oil
☐ 1 (1-ounce) jar crushed red pepper
☐ ¾-pound snow peas

3   tablespoons thawed orange juice concentrate
1   tablespoon lower-sodium soy sauce
1   teaspoon toasted sesame seeds
½   teaspoon grated fresh orange rind
1½   teaspoons dark sesame oil
⅛   teaspoon crushed red pepper
3   cups snow peas, trimmed (about ¾ pound)

1. Combine first 6 ingredients in a small bowl.
2. Heat a large nonstick skillet over medium-high heat; add orange juice mixture and snow peas. Cook 3 minutes, stirring often. Serve immediately. **Yield:** 4 servings (serving size: ½ cup).

Per serving: CALORIES 96; FAT 2.4g (sat 0.3g, mono 0.8g, poly 0.9g); PROTEIN 4.1g; CARB 15.1g; FIBER 3.4g; CHOL 0mg; IRON 3.8mg; SODIUM 139mg; CALC 59mg

Lemon-Herb Roasted Tomatoes

prep: 5 minutes • **cook:** 8 minutes   *PointsPlus* value per serving: 1

Grocery List

☐ 2 pints grape tomatoes
☐ 1 small lemon
☐ 1 (1-ounce) jar dried thyme
☐ Check staples: olive oil, pepper, salt

2   pints grape tomatoes
2   teaspoons olive oil
½   teaspoon grated fresh lemon rind
1   teaspoon fresh lemon juice
¾   teaspoon dried thyme
½   teaspoon freshly ground black pepper
¼   teaspoon salt

1. Preheat oven to 475°.
2. Rinse tomatoes, and pat dry with paper towels; place in a large bowl.
3. Gently stir in oil and remaining ingredients. Place tomato mixture in a single layer on a large jelly-roll pan.
4. Bake at 475° for 5 minutes. Gently shake pan, and bake an additional 3 to 5 minutes or until tomato skins are blistered and beginning to pop. **Yield:** 4 servings (serving size: ¾ cup).

Per serving: CALORIES 49; FAT 2.7g (sat 0.4g, mono 1.7g, poly 0.5g); PROTEIN 1.4g; CARB 6.4g; FIBER 2.1g; CHOL 0mg; IRON 0.6mg; SODIUM 153mg; CALC 20mg

Quick Sweet Potato Casserole

prep: 10 minutes • **cook:** 13 minutes

PointsPlus value per serving: 6

Grocery List

- ☐ 2 pounds sweet potatoes
- ☐ 1 box light stick butter
- ☐ 1 (1-ounce) jar ground nutmeg
- ☐ 1 (2-ounce) bag chopped pecans
- ☐ Maple syrup
- ☐ Check staples: salt, pepper, cooking spray

 4 sweet potatoes (about 2 pounds)
1½ tablespoons light stick butter
 ¼ teaspoon salt
 ⅛ teaspoon ground nutmeg
 ⅛ teaspoon freshly ground black pepper
Cooking spray
 ¼ cup chopped pecans
 3 tablespoons maple syrup

1. Scrub sweet potatoes; pat dry, and pierce several times with a small knife. Microwave potatoes at HIGH 10 minutes or until tender; cool slightly.
2. Peel potatoes, and place in a medium bowl. Add butter and next 3 ingredients. Beat potato mixture with a mixer at medium speed until smooth; spoon into a 1-quart glass or ceramic baking dish coated with cooking spray. Sprinkle with pecans, and drizzle with maple syrup.
3. Preheat broiler.
4. Broil 6 inches from heat 3 to 4 minutes or until nuts are golden. Serve immediately. **Yield:** 6 servings (serving size: ½ cup).

Per serving: CALORIES 236; FAT 5.1g (sat 1.2g, mono 1.9g, poly 1g); PROTEIN 2.8g; CARB 44.9g; FIBER 5.2g; CHOL 4mg; IRON 1.1mg; SODIUM 174mg; CALC 34mg

Buttermilk-Chive Mashed Potatoes

prep: 3 minutes • **cook:** 8 minutes

PointsPlus value per serving: 3

Grocery List

- ☐ 1 carton low-fat buttermilk
- ☐ 1 (8-ounce) carton reduced-fat sour cream
- ☐ 1 small tub yogurt-based spread
- ☐ 1 (22-ounce) package frozen mashed potatoes
- ☐ 1 bunch chives
- ☐ Check staple: pepper

2⅓ cups low-fat buttermilk
 ½ cup reduced-fat sour cream
 3 tablespoons yogurt-based spread
 ½ teaspoon freshly ground black pepper
 1 (22-ounce) package frozen mashed potatoes
 ¼ cup chopped fresh chives

1. Combine first 5 ingredients in a large microwave-safe serving bowl. Cover and microwave at HIGH 5 minutes; stir well. Microwave at HIGH 3 to 5 minutes or until thoroughly heated. Stir in chives. **Yield:** 11 servings (serving size: about ½ cup).

Per serving: CALORIES 131; FAT 4.8g (sat 1.8g, mono 2.5g, poly 0.3g); PROTEIN 4g; CARB 17.6g; FIBER 1.6g; CHOL 11mg; IRON 0.3mg; SODIUM 89mg; CALC 73mg

Cajun Potato Pancakes

prep: 3 minutes • **cook:** 10 minutes   *PointsPlus* value per serving: 3

These put a Louisiana-style spin on latkes. For traditional latkes, omit the Cajun seasoning, and serve with sour cream and hot sauce.

2	cups refrigerated shredded hash brown potatoes
2	large eggs
1½	tablespoons all-purpose flour
2	tablespoons finely chopped onion
4	teaspoons minced seeded jalapeño pepper (1 small pepper)
½	teaspoon Cajun seasoning
¼	teaspoon salt
2	tablespoons canola oil, divided
½	cup reduced-fat sour cream (optional)
	Hot sauce (optional)

1. Pat potatoes dry with paper towels. Place eggs in a medium bowl; stir with a whisk until lightly beaten. Add potatoes, flour, and next 4 ingredients.

2. Heat 1 tablespoon oil in a large nonstick skillet over medium heat. Drop half of batter by heaping tablespoonfuls into oil, spreading into 2-inch circles. Cook 3 minutes or until lightly browned. Turn pancakes over; cook 2 minutes or until potatoes are done. Drain on paper towels; keep warm. Repeat procedure with 1 tablespoon oil and remaining half of batter. Top pancakes with sour cream and hot sauce, if desired. **Yield:** 7 servings (serving size: 2 pancakes).

Per serving: CALORIES 104; FAT 5.5g (sat 0.7g, mono 3.1g, poly 1.3g); PROTEIN 2.6g; CARB 10.9g; FIBER 1.3g; CHOL 60mg; IRON 0.8mg; SODIUM 175mg; CALC 9mg

pictured on page 120

Pesto-Vegetable Medley

prep: 8 minutes • **cook:** 15 minutes   *PointsPlus* value per serving: 3

2 pounds red potatoes, unpeeled and halved (or quartered if large)
1 (12-ounce) package pretrimmed green beans
Cooking spray
1 pint grape tomatoes
5 tablespoons commercial pesto
¾ teaspoon salt
¼ teaspoon freshly ground black pepper

1. Place potatoes in a Dutch oven or large saucepan, and cover with water. Bring to a boil; reduce heat, cover, and cook 6 minutes. Add green beans; cook 8 minutes or until potatoes are tender and beans are crisp-tender. Drain; place potatoes and green beans in a large serving bowl, and set aside.

2. Wipe pan with a paper towel. Spray pan with cooking spray, and place over medium heat. Add tomatoes, and sauté 1 to 2 minutes or until tomatoes begin to brown slightly. Add to potatoes and green beans.

3. Combine pesto, salt, and pepper. Spoon over vegetable mixture, and toss gently to coat. Serve warm or at room temperature. **Yield:** 12 servings (serving size: 1 cup).

Per serving: CALORIES 100; FAT 3.2g (sat 0.8g, mono 1.8g, poly 0.3g); PROTEIN 3.3g; CARB 15.5g; FIBER 2.7g; CHOL 2mg; IRON 1.1mg; SODIUM 202mg; CALC 67mg

Grocery List

- ☐ 2 pounds red potatoes
- ☐ 1 (12-ounce) package green beans
- ☐ 1 pint grape tomatoes
- ☐ 1 (8.1-ounce) jar pesto
- ☐ Check staples: cooking spray, salt, pepper

pictured on page 118

Grilled Okra

prep: 10 minutes • **cook:** 8 minutes • **other:** 30 minutes

PointsPlus value per serving: 2

16 (12-inch) wooden skewers
1 pound small okra pods
1 tablespoon extra-virgin olive oil
1 teaspoon minced garlic
½ teaspoon salt
½ teaspoon freshly ground black pepper

1. Soak skewers in water 30 minutes.

2. Preheat grill to medium-high heat.

3. Divide okra among skewers (thread okra with 2 skewers to ease grilling). Combine olive oil and next 3 ingredients; brush over okra.

4. Grill 4 to 6 minutes on each side or until crisp-tender. Serve immediately.

Yield: 4 servings (serving size: 2 skewers).

Per serving: CALORIES 67; FAT 3.6g (sat 0.5g, mono 2.5g, poly 0.5g); PROTEIN 2.4g; CARB 8.4g; FIBER 3.7g; CHOL 0mg; IRON 0.9mg; SODIUM 300mg; CALC 94mg

Grocery List

- ☐ Wooden skewers
- ☐ 1 pound okra
- ☐ Check staples: olive oil, garlic, salt, pepper

Creamed Spinach

prep: 7 minutes • **cook:** 15 minutes   *PointsPlus* **value per serving: 4**

We used light butter, light cream cheese, and reduced-fat white cheddar cheese to decrease the fat, but not the flavor, in this comforting side dish.

Cooking spray
2 (12-ounce) bags fresh baby spinach
1 tablespoon light stick butter
⅓ cup finely chopped onion
2 teaspoons minced garlic
1 tablespoon all-purpose flour
4 ounces tub-style light cream cheese, softened (about ½ cup)
2 ounces reduced-fat shredded white cheddar cheese (about ½ cup)
¼ cup fat-free milk
¼ teaspoon freshly ground black pepper
¼ teaspoon hot sauce

1. Heat a large Dutch oven over medium-high heat; coat pan with cooking spray. Add spinach; sauté 5 minutes or until wilted. Drain spinach in a colander, pressing spinach with back of a spoon to remove as much moisture as possible.
2. Melt butter in pan; sauté onion and garlic over medium heat 3 minutes or until tender. Add flour, and cook 1 minute, stirring constantly. Add cheeses and milk; cook 2 minutes or until cheeses melt, stirring constantly. Add spinach; cook 3 minutes or until spinach is thoroughly heated. Remove from heat; stir in pepper and hot sauce. **Yield:** 4 servings (serving size: about ½ cup).

Per serving: CALORIES 159; FAT 7g (sat 4.4g, mono 1.2g, poly 0.3g); PROTEIN 11.5g; CARB 12g; FIBER 4.3g; CHOL 24mg; IRON 5.6mg; SODIUM 388mg; CALC 302mg

Zucchini with Pine Nuts and Lemon

prep: 6 minutes • **cook:** 12 minutes   *PointsPlus* value per serving: 1

    2   teaspoons extra-virgin olive oil
    Cooking spray
    3   medium zucchini, cut into ½-inch cubes
    1   tablespoon pine nuts, toasted
    2   teaspoons fresh lemon juice
    ½   teaspoon kosher salt
    ¼   teaspoon dried thyme
    ⅛   teaspoon coarsely ground black pepper

1. Heat oil in a large nonstick skillet coated with cooking spray over medium heat. Add zucchini; sauté 11 minutes or until tender. Stir in pine nuts and remaining ingredients. **Yield:** 5 servings (serving size: ½ cup).

Per serving: CALORIES 47; FAT 3.2g (sat 0.4g, mono 0.8g, poly 0.9g); PROTEIN 1.7g; CARB 4.4g; FIBER 1.4g; CHOL 0mg; IRON 0.5mg; SODIUM 200mg; CALC 19mg

Grocery List

☐ 3 medium zucchini
☐ 1 (2.25-ounce) bag pine nuts
☐ 1 lemon
☐ 1 (1-ounce) bottle dried thyme
☐ Check staples: olive oil, cooking spray, kosher salt, pepper

Bulgur-Pistachio Pilaf

prep: 4 minutes • **cook:** 18 minutes   *PointsPlus* value per serving: 4

Season this fiber-filled grain with mint and pistachios, and serve with grilled lamb, lemon chicken, or any other Mediterranean main dish.

    1   cup uncooked bulgur wheat
    ¾   cup fat-free, lower-sodium chicken broth
    ¾   cup water
    1   tablespoon light stick butter
    ½   teaspoon salt
    ½   teaspoon freshly ground black pepper
    ¼   cup chopped dry-roasted pistachios
    1   teaspoon dried mint flakes

1. Heat a large nonstick skillet over medium-high heat. Add bulgur wheat, and cook 4 minutes or until toasted, stirring constantly. Add broth and next 4 ingredients. Bring to a boil; cover, reduce heat, and simmer over medium-low heat 12 minutes or until liquid is absorbed. Remove from heat. Stir in pistachios and mint.
Yield: 5 servings (serving size: about ½ cup).

Per serving: CALORIES 146; FAT 4.5g (sat 1.1g, mono 1.5g, poly 1g); PROTEIN 5.3g; CARB 23.6g; FIBER 5.9g; CHOL 3mg; IRON 1.1mg; SODIUM 343mg; CALC 19mg

Grocery List

☐ 1 (18-ounce) package bulgur wheat
☐ 1 (14-ounce) can fat-free, lower-sodium chicken broth
☐ 1 box light stick butter
☐ 1 (4-ounce) bag dry-roasted pistachios
☐ 1 (1-ounce) bottle dried mint flakes
☐ Check staples: salt, pepper

Roasted Red Pepper Couscous

prep: 3 minutes • **cook:** 2 minutes • **other:** 5 minutes

PointsPlus value per serving: 3

1   cup water
⅔   cup uncooked couscous
2   teaspoons red wine vinegar
2   teaspoons olive oil
½   teaspoon bottled minced roasted garlic
¼   teaspoon freshly ground black pepper
⅛   teaspoon salt
½   cup drained bottled roasted red bell peppers, chopped
2   ounces crumbled feta cheese (about ½ cup)
¼   cup chopped fresh basil

1. Bring 1 cup water to a boil in a medium saucepan; gradually stir in couscous. Remove from heat; cover and let stand 5 minutes.
2. Combine vinegar and next 4 ingredients in a small bowl, stirring with a whisk. Add dressing, roasted bell peppers, cheese, and basil to couscous; fluff with a fork. **Yield:** 6 servings (serving size: ½ cup).

Per serving: CALORIES 112; FAT 3.8g (sat 1.3g, mono 1.5g, poly 0.5g); PROTEIN 4.9g; CARB 16.2g; FIBER 0.8g; CHOL 7mg; IRON 0.7mg; SODIUM 223mg; CALC 33mg

Grocery List

- ☐ 1 (10-ounce) box couscous
- ☐ Red wine vinegar
- ☐ 1 jar minced roasted garlic
- ☐ 1 (12-ounce) jar roasted red bell peppers
- ☐ 1 (4-ounce) container crumbled feta cheese
- ☐ 1 bunch basil
- ☐ Check staples: olive oil, pepper, salt

Herbed Cheese Grits

prep: 2 minutes • **cook:** 11 minutes   *PointsPlus* value per serving: 3

The light garlic-and-herbs spreadable cheese adds flavor and creaminess to plain grits for a quick side to serve with chicken, fish, or steak.

2   cups fat-free, lower-sodium chicken broth
½   cup uncooked quick-cooking grits
¼   cup light garlic-and-herbs spreadable cheese
¼   teaspoon freshly ground black pepper

1. Bring broth to a boil in a medium saucepan over medium-high heat.
2. Slowly stir in grits; cover, reduce heat, and simmer 5 minutes or until grits are thick, stirring occasionally.
3. Stir in cheese and pepper. Cook 1 to 2 minutes or until cheese melts, stirring occasionally. Serve immediately. **Yield:** 4 servings (serving size: ½ cup).

Per serving: CALORIES 75; FAT 2.2g (sat 1.5g, mono 0g, poly 0g); PROTEIN 3.2g; CARB 16.1g; FIBER 0.3g; CHOL 10mg; IRON 0.8mg; SODIUM 285mg; CALC 2mg

Grocery List

- ☐ 1 (32-ounce) carton fat-free, lower-sodium chicken broth
- ☐ 1 (18.4-ounce) box quick-cooking grits
- ☐ 1 (6.5-ounce) package light garlic-and-herbs spreadable cheese
- ☐ Check staple: pepper

Curried Rice with Onions and Cashews

prep: 12 minutes • **cook:** 23 minutes   *PointsPlus* value per serving: 4

Basmati rice has a nutlike flavor and aroma. Toasting the mustard seeds, turmeric, and curry releases their flavors, infusing the rice with a warm spiciness.

⅔ cup uncooked basmati rice
1 tablespoon canola oil
½ teaspoon mustard seeds
½ teaspoon ground turmeric
½ teaspoon curry powder
2 cups sliced onion
1 tablespoon grated peeled fresh ginger
1 jalapeño pepper, seeded and minced
½ teaspoon salt
½ teaspoon sugar
2 tablespoons fresh lime juice
¼ cup chopped salted dry-roasted cashews

1. Cook rice according to package directions, omitting salt and fat.
2. Heat oil in a medium saucepan over medium-high heat. Add mustard seeds; cover and cook 1 minute or until seeds pop. Reduce heat to medium, and stir in turmeric and curry. Add onion, ginger, and jalapeño; cook 13 minutes or until onion is tender and lightly browned, stirring frequently.
3. Add salt, sugar, and cooked rice to onion mixture, stirring well. Cook 3 minutes or until thoroughly heated. Stir in lime juice, and top with cashews. **Yield:** 5 servings (serving size: ½ cup).

Per serving: CALORIES 134; FAT 6.2g (sat 0.9g, mono 3.7g, poly 1.4g); PROTEIN 2.5g; CARB 18.2g; FIBER 1.3g; CHOL 0mg; IRON 0.8mg; SODIUM 278mg; CALC 18mg

Grocery List

- ☐ 1 (12-ounce) package basmati rice
- ☐ 1 (1-ounce) bottle mustard seeds
- ☐ 1 (1-ounce) bottle ground turmeric
- ☐ 1 (1-ounce) bottle curry powder
- ☐ 2 large onions
- ☐ 1 small piece fresh ginger
- ☐ 1 jalapeño pepper
- ☐ 1 lime
- ☐ 1 (8-ounce) container dry-roasted cashews
- ☐ Check staples: canola oil, salt, sugar

pictured on page 121

Risotto with Fresh Mozzarella, Tomatoes, and Basil

prep: 9 minutes • **cook:** 26 minutes   *PointsPlus* value per serving: 3

The highlight of this microwave risotto is the fresh mozzarella. Try not to overstir when adding the mozzarella, or the cheese will melt too much.

Grocery List

- ☐ 1 onion
- ☐ 1 (32-ounce) carton organic vegetable broth
- ☐ 1 (12-ounce) package Arborio rice
- ☐ Dry white wine
- ☐ 1 bunch basil
- ☐ 1 pint grape tomatoes
- ☐ 1 (8-ounce) package mozzarella cheese
- ☐ Check staples: butter, garlic, cooking spray, salt

¾   cup chopped onion
2   teaspoons butter
2   garlic cloves, minced
Cooking spray
4   cups organic vegetable broth
1   cup uncooked Arborio rice
½   cup dry white wine
¼   cup chopped fresh basil
½   teaspoon salt
1   pint grape tomatoes, halved
1   ounce (¼-inch) diced fresh mozzarella cheese (about ¼ cup)
Fresh basil leaves (optional)

1. Combine first 3 ingredients in an 11 x 7–inch glass or ceramic baking dish coated with cooking spray. Microwave, uncovered, at HIGH 2 minutes or until tender.
2. Microwave broth in a glass bowl at HIGH 4 minutes or until hot. Stir rice and hot broth into onion mixture; microwave, uncovered, at HIGH 10 minutes. Stir in wine; microwave at HIGH 10 minutes or until liquid is almost absorbed, stirring twice. Stir in basil, salt, and tomatoes. Gently fold in cheese. Garnish with basil leaves, if desired. Serve immediately. **Yield:** 8 servings (serving size: ½ cup).

Per serving: CALORIES 123; FAT 2.1g (sat 1.1g, mono 0.5g, poly 0.1g); PROTEIN 2.9g; CARB 22.7g; FIBER 1.2g; CHOL 5mg; IRON 0.4mg; SODIUM 515mg; CALC 29mg

Breads

Pepperoni Pizza Pinwheels

prep: 12 minutes • **cook:** 20 minutes

PointsPlus value per serving: 2

Serve these cheesy pinwheels as a salad accompaniment.

1 (11-ounce) can refrigerated French bread dough
Cooking spray
¼ cup sun-dried tomato pesto
18 slices turkey pepperoni
2 ounces preshredded part-skim mozzarella cheese (about ½ cup)

1. Preheat oven to 350°.
2. Unroll dough onto a work surface; lightly coat dough with cooking spray.
3. Spoon pesto onto dough, spreading to edges. Place pepperoni slices over pesto, and sprinkle with cheese. Starting at a long edge, roll up dough tightly, jelly-roll fashion; pinch seam to seal (do not seal ends of roll). Using a serrated knife, cut roll into 16 slices. Place slices, cut sides down, on a baking sheet coated with cooking spray.
4. Bake at 350° for 20 minutes or until golden brown. **Yield:** 16 pinwheels (serving size: 1 pinwheel).

Per serving: CALORIES 65; FAT 1.7g (sat 0.7g, mono 0.1g, poly 0.1g); PROTEIN 3.2g; CARB 9.7g; FIBER 0.3g; CHOL 5mg; IRON 0.7mg; SODIUM 209mg; CALC 23mg

Herb-Grilled Flatbread

prep: 6 minutes • **cook:** 4 minutes

PointsPlus value per serving: 3

1 tablespoon olive oil
2 teaspoons chopped fresh rosemary
2 teaspoons chopped fresh thyme
¼ teaspoon salt
¼ teaspoon freshly ground black pepper
3 garlic cloves, minced
2 (6-inch) wheat flatbread rounds
Cooking spray

1. Preheat grill to medium heat.
2. Combine first 6 ingredients in a small bowl.
3. Spray both sides of bread with cooking spray. Place bread on grill rack; grill 2 minutes. Turn and spread olive oil mixture on grilled side of bread. Grill 2 minutes or until thoroughly heated. Cut each round into 8 wedges. **Yield:** 4 servings (serving size: 4 wedges).

Per serving: CALORIES 104; FAT 3.4g (sat 0.5g, mono 1.2g, poly 0.2g); PROTEIN 3.2g; CARB 16g; FIBER 3.2g; CHOL 0mg; IRON 1.1mg; SODIUM 211mg; CALC 27mg

Three-Seed Breadsticks

prep: 10 minutes • **cook:** 8 minutes   *PointsPlus* value per serving: 2

Serve these crunchy breadsticks instead of crackers with a bowl of soup or a mixed green salad. Store in an airtight container to keep them crisp.

1   (7.5-ounce) can refrigerated buttermilk biscuits
¾   cup oven-toasted rice cereal, coarsely crushed
1   tablespoon caraway seeds
1   tablespoon sesame seeds
1   tablespoon poppy seeds
1   large egg white, lightly beaten
Cooking spray
1   teaspoon kosher salt

1. Preheat oven to 450°.
2. Cut each biscuit in half horizontally, and roll each half into a pencil-thin stick. Combine cereal and seeds in a shallow dish, stirring well. Brush biscuit sticks with egg white; roll in cereal mixture. Place breadsticks 2 inches apart on a large baking sheet coated with cooking spray, and sprinkle with salt.
3. Bake at 450° for 8 to 10 minutes or until lightly browned. **Yield:** 10 servings (serving size: 2 breadsticks).

Per serving: CALORIES 73; FAT 1.4g (sat 0.2g, mono 0.3g, poly 0.5g); PROTEIN 2.6g; CARB 12.6g; FIBER 0.4g; CHOL 0mg; IRON 0.9mg; SODIUM 376mg; CALC 26mg

Grocery List

☐ 1 (7.5-ounce) can buttermilk biscuits
☐ 1 (12.8-ounce) box oven-toasted rice cereal
☐ 1 (1-ounce) bottle caraway seeds
☐ 1 (1-ounce) bottle sesame seeds
☐ 1 (1-ounce) bottle poppy seeds
☐ Check staples: eggs, cooking spray, kosher salt

Green-Chile Corn Bread

prep: 9 minutes • **cook:** 28 minutes • **other:** 5 minutes

PointsPlus value per serving: 4

This golden corn bread cooks in a baking pan, so you don't have to pull out your heavy cast-iron skillet.

4.5 ounces all-purpose flour (about 1 cup)
1 cup stone-ground yellow cornmeal
¾ teaspoon baking powder
½ teaspoon salt
¼ teaspoon baking soda
1 cup low-fat buttermilk
2 tablespoons canola oil
2 large eggs, lightly beaten
1 large egg white
1 ounce shredded reduced-fat colby-Jack cheese (about ¼ cup)
1 (4.5-ounce) can chopped green chiles, drained
Cooking spray

1. Preheat oven to 425°.

2. Weigh or lightly spoon flour into a dry measuring cup; level with a knife. Combine flour and next 4 ingredients in a large bowl. Combine buttermilk and next 3 ingredients in another bowl, stirring with a whisk. Add buttermilk mixture to flour mixture, stirring just until moist. Gently fold in cheese and green chiles; pour batter into a 9-inch square metal baking pan coated with cooking spray.

3. Bake at 425° for 28 minutes or until golden. Let stand 5 minutes before cutting into squares. **Yield:** 9 servings (serving size: 1 square).

Per serving: CALORIES 170; FAT 5.2g (sat 1.1g, mono 1.8g, poly 1.7g); PROTEIN 6.3g; CARB 24.3g; FIBER 1.5g; CHOL 49mg; IRON 1.6mg; SODIUM 499mg; CALC 162mg

Caramelized Red Onion, Rosemary, and Asiago Focaccia

prep: 16 minutes • **cook:** 34 minutes • **other:** 2 minutes

PointsPlus value per serving: 4

Impress company with this easy, colorful bread. Coarse kosher salt adds a nice contrast to the chewy texture, but a light sprinkle of regular table salt is fine.

Grocery List
- ☐ 1 large red onion
- ☐ 1 (13.8-ounce) can refrigerated pizza crust dough
- ☐ 1 bunch rosemary
- ☐ 1 (8-ounce) container finely shredded Asiago cheese
- ☐ Check staples: olive oil, cooking spray, pepper, kosher salt

2½ teaspoons olive oil, divided
1 large red onion, halved lengthwise and thinly sliced
1 (13.8-ounce) can refrigerated pizza crust dough
Cooking spray
1 tablespoon chopped fresh rosemary
½ teaspoon freshly ground black pepper
⅛ teaspoon kosher salt
2 ounces finely shredded Asiago cheese (about ½ cup)

1. Preheat oven to 450°.
2. Heat 1 teaspoon oil in a large nonstick skillet over medium-high heat. Add onion; sauté 6 minutes. Reduce heat to medium; cook 15 minutes or until deep golden brown. Remove from heat.
3. Unroll dough onto a baking sheet coated with cooking spray. Pat dough into a 14 x 10–inch rectangle. Spread 1½ teaspoons oil over dough; sprinkle with rosemary, pepper, and salt. Bake at 450° for 8 minutes.
4. Sprinkle onion and cheese over crust. Bake an additional 5 minutes or until golden brown and cheese melts. Cool on a wire rack 2 minutes; cut into 8 equal pieces. **Yield:** 8 servings (serving size: 1 piece).

Per serving: CALORIES 175; FAT 5g (sat 1.4g, mono 1.0g, poly 0.2g); PROTEIN 6.4g; CARB 25.4g; FIBER 1g; CHOL 6mg; IRON 1.3mg; SODIUM 374mg; CALC 70mg

Almond–Poppy Seed Swirls

prep: 13 minutes • **cook:** 15 minutes • **other:** 12 hours and 35 minutes

PointsPlus value per serving: 5

Frozen bread dough allows you to serve ooey-gooey poppy seed rolls in half the time of homemade yeast rolls. Just remember to plan ahead for thawing the dough.

- 1 (1-pound) loaf frozen white bread dough
- 3 tablespoons light stick butter, softened
- 3 tablespoons brown sugar
- 1½ tablespoons poppy seeds
- ¼ teaspoon almond extract
- Cooking spray
- ¾ cup powdered sugar
- 4 teaspoons fat-free milk
- 3 tablespoons sliced almonds, toasted

1. Thaw dough in refrigerator 12 hours.

2. Place dough on a lightly floured surface; let rest 5 minutes. Pat or roll dough into a 15 x 8–inch rectangle (about ¼ inch thick). Spread butter over dough, leaving a ½-inch border. Combine brown sugar, poppy seeds, and almond extract; sprinkle over butter. Starting at long edge, roll up dough tightly, jelly-roll fashion; pinch seam to seal (do not seal ends of roll).

3. Place a long piece of dental floss or string under dough 1¼ inches from end of roll. Cross ends of string over top of roll; slowly pull ends to cut through dough. Place slice, cut side up, on a baking sheet coated with cooking spray. Coat slice with cooking spray. Repeat procedure with remaining roll, placing slices 2 inches apart on prepared pan. Cover and let rise in a warm place (85°), free from drafts, 30 minutes or until doubled in size.

4. Preheat oven to 375°.

5. Bake at 375° for 15 minutes or until lightly browned. Combine powdered sugar and milk, stirring until smooth. Place glaze in a small zip-top plastic bag; seal. Snip a tiny hole in one corner of bag; drizzle glaze over warm rolls, and sprinkle with almonds. **Yield:** 12 rolls (serving size: 1 roll).

Per serving: CALORIES 170; FAT 4.5g (sat 1.1g, mono 0.1g, poly 0.3g); PROTEIN 4.8g; CARB 29.8g; FIBER 1.4g; CHOL 5mg; IRON 1.6mg; SODIUM 230mg; CALC 32mg

pictured on page 122

Parmesan-Basil Biscuits

prep: 12 minutes • **cook:** 10 minutes   *PointsPlus* value per serving: 3

These quick and easy biscuits received rave reviews in our Test Kitchen. We preferred the appearance of finely shredded fresh Parmesan cheese on top of the biscuits, even though grated Parmesan is used in the biscuit dough. If you don't have fresh Parmesan, it's fine to top the biscuits with grated Parmesan cheese.

Grocery List

☐ 1 (8-ounce) container grated Parmesan cheese
☐ 1 bunch basil
☐ 1 carton low-fat buttermilk
☐ 1 small block fresh Parmesan cheese
☐ Check staples: flour, baking powder, baking soda, salt, butter, cooking spray

4.5 ounces all-purpose flour (about 1 cup)
  1 teaspoon baking powder
  ¼ teaspoon baking soda
  ¼ teaspoon salt
  3 tablespoons chilled butter, cut into small pieces
  ¼ cup grated Parmesan cheese
  2 tablespoons chopped fresh basil
  ½ cup low-fat buttermilk
Cooking spray
  1 tablespoon finely shredded fresh Parmesan cheese

1. Preheat oven to 425°.

2. Weigh or lightly spoon flour into a dry measuring cup; level with a knife. Combine flour and next 3 ingredients in a bowl. Cut in butter with a pastry blender or 2 knives until mixture resembles coarse meal. Stir in grated Parmesan cheese and basil. Add buttermilk, stirring just until moist.

3. Spoon dough into 8 mounds on a baking sheet coated with cooking spray. Lightly coat tops of biscuits with cooking spray, and sprinkle with finely shredded Parmesan cheese.

4. Bake at 425° for 10 to 12 minutes or until golden. Serve immediately. **Yield:** 8 biscuits (serving size: 1 biscuit).

Per serving: CALORIES 114; FAT 5.4g (sat 3.4g, mono 1.4g, poly 0.3g); PROTEIN 3.4g; CARB 12.8g; FIBER 0.5g; CHOL 15mg; IRON 0.8mg; SODIUM 259mg; CALC 88mg

Corn and Zucchini Muffins

prep: 15 minutes • **cook:** 15 minutes   *PointsPlus* value per serving: 4

These savory muffins are a perfect accompaniment to soup or chili.

Grocery List

- ☐ 1 bag whole-wheat flour
- ☐ 1 bag self-rising cornmeal mix
- ☐ 1 carton 1% low-fat milk
- ☐ 1 (6-ounce) carton plain fat-free yogurt
- ☐ 1 large zucchini
- ☐ 3 small ears corn
- ☐ 1 small onion
- ☐ Check staples: sugar, baking soda, salt, canola oil, eggs, cooking spray

4.75 ounces whole-wheat flour (about 1 cup)
   1 cup self-rising cornmeal mix
   2 tablespoons sugar
  ¼ teaspoon baking soda
  ¼ teaspoon salt
  ⅓ cup 1% low-fat milk
   3 tablespoons canola oil
   1 (6-ounce) carton plain fat-free yogurt
   1 large egg
   1 cup shredded zucchini
  ¾ cup fresh corn kernels (3 small ears)
   2 tablespoons minced onion
     Cooking spray

1. Preheat oven to 425°.

2. Weigh or lightly spoon flour and cornmeal mix into dry measuring cups; level with a knife. Combine flour, cornmeal mix, sugar, baking soda, and salt in a large bowl; stir with a whisk. Make a well in center of mixture. Combine milk and next 3 ingredients in a small bowl; stir with a whisk. Add zucchini, corn, and onion; stir. Add vegetable mixture to flour mixture, stirring just until moist.

3. Spoon batter into 12 muffin cups coated with cooking spray; coat batter with cooking spray. Bake at 425° for 15 minutes or until muffins spring back when touched lightly in center. **Yield:** 12 servings (serving size: 1 muffin).

Per serving: CALORIES 149; FAT 4.8g (sat 0.5g, mono 2.5g, poly 1.2g); PROTEIN 4.6g; CARB 23.2g; FIBER 2.1g; CHOL 18mg; IRON 1.2mg; SODIUM 292mg; CALC 53mg

pictured on page 123

Blueberry–Brown Sugar Muffins

prep: 10 minutes • **cook:** 24 minutes   *PointsPlus* value per serving: 4

These brown sugar–topped muffins use fresh or frozen blueberries, which are ranked by the USDA as the fruit having the highest level of antioxidants.

Grocery List
- [ ] 1 (16-ounce) carton plain low-fat yogurt
- [ ] 1 small lemon
- [ ] 1 pint fresh blueberries or 1 (10-ounce) package frozen blueberries
- [ ] Check staples: flour, sugar, baking powder, baking soda, salt, butter, eggs, cooking spray, brown sugar

7.9 ounces all-purpose flour (about 1¾ cups)
½ cup granulated sugar
1½ teaspoons baking powder
½ teaspoon baking soda
¼ teaspoon salt
1 cup plain low-fat yogurt
2 tablespoons butter, melted
1 large egg
1 teaspoon grated fresh lemon rind
1 cup fresh blueberries or frozen unsweetened blueberries
Cooking spray
1 tablespoon brown sugar

1. Preheat oven to 350°.
2. Weigh or lightly spoon flour into dry measuring cups; level with a knife. Combine flour and next 4 ingredients in a large bowl; stir well.
3. Combine yogurt and next 3 ingredients in a small bowl, stirring with a whisk until smooth. Add yogurt mixture to flour mixture, stirring just until moist. Gently fold in blueberries.
4. Place 12 paper muffin cup liners in muffin cups; coat liners with cooking spray. Spoon batter into prepared cups. Sprinkle with brown sugar. Bake at 350° for 24 minutes or until lightly browned and muffins spring back when touched lightly in center. **Yield:** 12 servings (serving size: 1 muffin).

Per serving: CALORIES 144; FAT 2.8g (sat 1.6g, mono 0.7g, poly 0.2g); PROTEIN 3.4g; CARB 26.3g; FIBER 0.8g; CHOL 24mg; IRON 1mg; SODIUM 196mg; CALC 74mg

Strawberry Muffins

prep: 18 minutes • **cook:** 22 minutes

PointsPlus value per serving: 4

These moist muffins will spoil quickly because of the fruit, so freeze leftover muffins in zip-top freezer bags. Heat them in the microwave for 15 seconds before serving.

7.5 ounces all-purpose flour (about 1⅔ cups)
½ cup granulated sugar
1 teaspoon baking soda
¼ teaspoon salt
1 cup sliced fresh strawberries
⅔ cup low-fat buttermilk
¼ cup butter, melted
1 teaspoon vanilla extract
1 large egg
Cooking spray
1 tablespoon turbinado sugar

1. Preheat oven to 400°.
2. Weigh or lightly spoon flour into dry measuring cups; level with a knife. Combine flour and next 3 ingredients in a large bowl; stir well with a whisk. Add strawberries, gently tossing to coat.
3. Combine buttermilk and next 3 ingredients in a small bowl; stir with a whisk. Add to flour mixture, stirring just until moist. Spoon batter into 12 muffin cups coated with cooking spray. Sprinkle batter with turbinado sugar.
4. Bake at 400° for 22 minutes or until muffins spring back when touched lightly in center. Remove muffins from pans immediately; place on a wire rack. **Yield:** 12 muffins (serving size: 1 muffin).

Per serving: CALORIES 149; FAT 4.5g (sat 2.6g, mono 1.2g, poly 0.3g); PROTEIN 2.9g; CARB 24.3g; FIBER 0.7g; CHOL 28mg; IRON 1mg; SODIUM 201mg; CALC 24mg

Nectarine-Oatmeal Scones

prep: 14 minutes • **cook:** 20 minutes

PointsPlus value per serving: 5

Adding oats to the scones gives them a hearty, nutty flavor and also increases the fiber. We chose nectarines over peaches for this recipe because although the two fruits are similar in flavor, nectarines release less juice when baked. We tried substituting peaches, but the scones were too wet and gummy.

Grocery List

- ☐ 1 (18-ounce) canister old-fashioned rolled oats
- ☐ 1 carton low-fat buttermilk
- ☐ 3 small nectarines
- ☐ 1 (16-ounce) bag turbinado sugar
- ☐ Check staples: flour, sugar, baking powder, baking soda, salt, butter, cooking spray

5.6   ounces all-purpose flour (about 1¼ cups)
⅓   cup granulated sugar
2   teaspoons baking powder
½   teaspoon baking soda
¼   teaspoon salt
⅓   cup chilled butter, cut into small pieces
1   cup old-fashioned rolled oats
½   cup low-fat buttermilk
1½   cups chopped nectarines (about 3 small)
  Cooking spray
1   tablespoon turbinado sugar

1. Preheat oven to 425°.
2. Weigh or lightly spoon flour into dry measuring cups; level with a knife. Combine flour and next 4 ingredients in a large bowl. Cut in butter with a pastry blender or 2 knives until mixture resembles coarse meal. Stir in oats. Add buttermilk to flour mixture, stirring just until moist. Gently fold in nectarines.
3. Turn dough out onto a lightly floured surface; knead lightly 3 or 4 times with floured hands. Pat dough into a 7-inch circle on a baking sheet coated with cooking spray. Cut dough into 10 wedges, cutting into but not through dough (do not separate wedges). Lightly coat tops of scones with cooking spray; sprinkle with turbinado sugar. Bake at 425° for 20 minutes or until lightly browned.
Yield: 10 servings (serving size: 1 wedge).

Per serving: CALORIES 193; FAT 7g (sat 4g, mono 1.5g, poly 0.5g); PROTEIN 3.8g; CARB 30g; FIBER 2g; CHOL 17mg; IRON 1.3mg; SODIUM 276mg; CALC 79mg

Sunshine Scones

prep: 10 minutes • **cook:** 14 minutes

PointsPlus value per serving: 4

Cut into, but not completely through, the circles of dough to create wedges; do not separate. Keeping the wedges together allows them to bake as one large scone, making them moister than if they were baked separately. The wedges come apart easily after baking.

9	ounces all-purpose flour (about 2 cups)
¼	cup granulated sugar
2	teaspoons baking powder
½	teaspoon baking soda
¼	teaspoon salt
2	tablespoons chilled butter, cut into small pieces
⅔	cup light sour cream
½	cup low-fat buttermilk
1	tablespoon grated fresh lemon rind
	Cooking spray
2	teaspoons turbinado sugar

1. Preheat oven to 400°.

2. Weigh or lightly spoon flour into dry measuring cups; level with a knife. Combine flour and next 4 ingredients in a large bowl; cut in butter with a pastry blender or 2 knives until mixture resembles coarse meal.

3. Combine sour cream, buttermilk, and lemon rind in a small bowl; add to flour mixture, stirring just until moist.

4. Turn dough out onto a lightly floured surface; knead lightly 4 times. Divide dough in half, and pat each half into a 5½-inch circle on a baking sheet coated with cooking spray. Cut each circle into 6 wedges, cutting into but not through dough (do not separate wedges). Sprinkle with turbinado sugar. Bake at 400° for 14 minutes or until lightly browned. **Yield:** 12 servings (serving size: 1 scone).

Per serving: CALORIES 133; FAT 3.8g (sat 2.3g, mono 1.0g, poly 0.2g); PROTEIN 2.9g; CARB 21.9g; FIBER 0.6g; CHOL 11mg; IRON 1.1mg; SODIUM 212mg; CALC 75mg

Parmesan–Black Pepper Scones

prep: 23 minutes • **cook:** 24 minutes

PointsPlus value per serving: 5

Serve as a dinner bread or with fruit spread for a sweet-and-spicy breakfast.

Grocery List

- ☐ 1 (8-ounce) container preshredded fresh Parmesan cheese
- ☐ 1 carton low-fat buttermilk
- ☐ Check staples: flour, baking powder, sugar, pepper, salt, butter, egg, cooking spray

9   ounces all-purpose flour (about 2 cups)
1   tablespoon baking powder
2   teaspoons sugar
2   teaspoons freshly ground black pepper
½   teaspoon salt
3   tablespoons chilled butter, cut into small pieces
2   ounces shredded fresh Parmesan cheese (about ½ cup)
⅔   cup low-fat buttermilk
1   large egg
Cooking spray

1. Preheat oven to 400°.

2. Weigh or lightly spoon flour into dry measuring cups; level with a knife. Combine flour and next 4 ingredients in a large bowl; cut in butter with a pastry blender or 2 knives until mixture resembles coarse meal. Stir in cheese.

3. Combine buttermilk and egg in a small bowl, stirring with a whisk. Add to flour mixture, stirring just until moist.

4. Turn dough out onto a lightly floured surface; knead lightly 5 times with floured hands. Pat dough into an 8-inch circle on a baking sheet coated with cooking spray. Cut dough into 8 wedges, cutting into but not through dough. Coat lightly with cooking spray.

5. Bake at 400° for 24 minutes or until lightly browned. **Yield:** 8 scones (serving size: 1 scone).

Per serving: CALORIES 196; FAT 6.7g (sat 3.9g, mono 1.9g, poly 0.4g); PROTEIN 6.7g; CARB 26.9g; FIBER 1g; CHOL 42mg; IRON 1.9mg; SODIUM 474mg; CALC 199mg

Grocery List

- ☐ 1 (8-ounce) block ⅓-less-fat cream cheese
- ☐ 1 small orange
- ☐ 1 (1-ounce) bottle coconut extract
- ☐ 1 (6-ounce) carton piña colada–flavored low-fat yogurt
- ☐ 1 (7-ounce) bag flaked sweetened coconut
- ☐ 1 (8-ounce) can crushed pineapple in juice
- ☐ 1 (1-pound) box powdered sugar
- ☐ Check staples: flour, baking powder, baking soda, salt, butter, sugar, eggs, cooking spray

Tropical Tea Bread

prep: 9 minutes • **cook:** 58 minutes • **other:** 35 minutes

PointsPlus value per serving: 4

This flavorful, cakelike quick bread earned our Test Kitchen's highest rating. Since the tender loaf contains chunks of fruit, we recommend using a serrated knife to cut neat slices.

    4.5   ounces all-purpose flour (about 1 cup)
    ½   teaspoon baking powder
    ¼   teaspoon baking soda
    ¼   teaspoon salt
    4   ounces ⅓-less-fat cream cheese, softened (about ½ cup)
    ¼   cup butter, softened
    ⅔   cup granulated sugar
    1   large egg
    2¼   teaspoons grated fresh orange rind, divided
    ¼   teaspoon coconut extract
    1   (6-ounce) carton piña colada–flavored low-fat yogurt
    ⅓   cup flaked sweetened coconut, toasted
    ¼   cup canned crushed pineapple in juice, drained
          Cooking spray
    ⅓   cup powdered sugar
    2   teaspoons fresh orange juice

1. Preheat oven to 325°.

2. Weigh or lightly spoon flour into a dry measuring cup; level with a knife. Combine flour and next 3 ingredients in a small bowl. Combine cream cheese and butter in a large bowl; beat with a mixer at medium speed until well blended. Gradually add granulated sugar, and beat until light and fluffy. Add egg, 2 teaspoons orange rind, and coconut extract, beating just until blended. Add flour mixture to butter mixture alternately with yogurt, beginning and ending with flour mixture. Stir in coconut and pineapple.

3. Spoon batter into an 8 x 4–inch loaf pan coated with cooking spray. Bake at 325° for 58 minutes or until a wooden pick inserted in center comes out clean. Cool in pan 5 minutes on a wire rack. Remove from pan; cool completely on wire rack over wax paper.

4. Combine powdered sugar, ¼ teaspoon orange rind, and orange juice in a small bowl, stirring until smooth. Drizzle glaze over top of loaf. **Yield:** 14 servings (serving size: 1 slice).

Per serving: CALORIES 158; FAT 6.2g (sat 4g, mono 1.0g, poly 0.2g); PROTEIN 2.7g; CARB 23.5g; FIBER 0.4g; CHOL 30mg; IRON 0.6mg; SODIUM 153mg; CALC 36mg

Easy Rosemary Wheat Rolls

prep: 15 minutes • **cook:** 17 minutes • **other:** 1 hour and 25 minutes

PointsPlus value per serving: 3

Rosemary brings out the natural sweetness found in wheat. These rolls are best served warm from the oven.

  1   package dry yeast (about 2¼ teaspoons)
1¼   cups warm water (100° to 110°)
  2   tablespoons sugar
  2   tablespoons light stick butter, melted
  2   teaspoons minced fresh rosemary
1¼   teaspoons salt
  ½   teaspoon garlic powder
  1   large egg, lightly beaten
4.75 ounces whole-wheat flour (about 1 cup)
7.95 ounces bread flour (about 1⅔ cups)
      Cooking spray

1. Dissolve yeast in 1¼ cups warm water in a large bowl; let stand 10 minutes. Stir in sugar and next 5 ingredients.
2. Weigh or lightly spoon flours into dry measuring cups; level with a knife. Add whole-wheat flour to yeast mixture; stir until smooth. Gradually stir in bread flour to make a thick batter. Cover with plastic wrap, and let rise in a warm place (85°), free from drafts, 1 hour or until doubled in size. (Gently press two fingers into dough. If indentation remains, dough has risen enough.)
3. Stir batter down; spoon into 15 muffin cups coated with cooking spray. Cover and let rise in a warm place (85°) 15 to 20 minutes or until batter rises to top of muffin cups.
4. Preheat oven to 375°.
5. Uncover rolls, and bake at 375° for 17 to 20 minutes or until lightly browned. Serve warm. **Yield:** 15 rolls (serving size: 1 roll).

Per serving: CALORIES 102; FAT 1.6g (sat 0.7g, mono 0.2g, poly 0.2g); PROTEIN 3.7g; CARB 18.8g; FIBER 1.5g; CHOL 17mg; IRON 1.2mg; SODIUM 209mg; CALC 8mg

Grocery List

- [ ] 1 (3-packet) strip dry yeast
- [ ] 1 box light stick butter
- [ ] 1 bunch rosemary
- [ ] 1 (1-ounce) bottle garlic powder
- [ ] 1 small bag whole-wheat flour
- [ ] 1 small bag bread flour
- [ ] Check staples: sugar, salt, eggs, cooking spray

Grocery List

☐ 1 (3-packet) strip dry yeast
☐ Check staples: sugar, flour, salt, butter, cooking spray, baking soda, kosher salt

Soft Pretzels

prep: 41 minutes • **cook:** 19 minutes • **other:** 55 minutes

PointsPlus value per serving: 3

For the finishing touch, serve each pretzel warm from the oven with 1 tablespoon honey mustard for a total *PointsPlus* value of 4, if desired.

1	tablespoon sugar
1	package dry yeast (about 2¼ teaspoons)
1	cup warm water (100° to 110°)
13.5	ounces all-purpose flour, divided (about 3 cups)
1	teaspoon salt
1	tablespoon butter, melted
	Cooking spray
4	cups water
2	tablespoons baking soda
¾	teaspoon kosher salt, divided

1. Dissolve sugar and yeast in 1 cup warm water in a small bowl; let stand 5 minutes. Weigh or lightly spoon flour into dry measuring cups; level with a knife. Combine 1½ cups flour and salt in a large bowl. Add butter, yeast mixture, and 1½ cups flour, stirring until a soft dough forms.

2. Turn dough out onto a lightly floured surface, and knead until smooth and elastic (about 5 minutes). Place dough in a large bowl coated with cooking spray, turning to coat top. Cover and let rise in a warm place (85°), free from drafts, 40 minutes or until doubled in size. (Gently press two fingers into dough. If indentation remains, the dough has risen enough.)

3. Punch dough down; divide into 12 equal portions. Cover and let rest 10 minutes on a lightly floured surface. Shape each portion of dough into an 18-inch long rope with tapered ends; twist each rope into a pretzel shape.

4. Preheat oven to 450°.

5. Combine 4 cups water and baking soda in a large nonaluminum Dutch oven; bring to a boil. Add 4 pretzels; cook 1 minute, turning once (do not overcrowd pan). Remove pretzels with a slotted spoon; shake off excess water. Place pretzels on a baking sheet coated with cooking spray; sprinkle ¼ teaspoon kosher salt over pretzels. Repeat procedure twice with remaining pretzels and salt.

6. Bake pretzels at 450° for 10 minutes or until golden brown. Remove from pans to wire racks. **Yield:** 12 servings (serving size: 1 pretzel).

Per serving: CALORIES 128; FAT 1.3g (sat 0.6g, mono 0.5g, poly 0.1g); PROTEIN 3.5g; CARB 25.1g; FIBER 1g; CHOL 3mg; IRON 1.6mg; SODIUM 374mg; CALC 5mg

Cranberry-Walnut Bread

prep: 19 minutes • **cook:** 30 minutes • **other:** 1 hour and 35 minutes

PointsPlus value per serving: 4

Your whole house will smell like the holidays when this bread is baking.

⅓   cup sugar
1   package dry yeast (about 2¼ teaspoons)
1   cup warm 2% reduced-fat milk (100° to 110°)
½   teaspoon salt
2   tablespoons butter, melted
12.4   ounces all-purpose flour, divided (about 2¾ cups)
½   cup dried cranberries
⅓   cup chopped walnuts
Cooking spray

1. Dissolve sugar and yeast in warm milk in a large bowl; let stand 5 minutes. Add salt; stir to dissolve. Stir in butter.
2. Weigh or lightly spoon flour into dry measuring cups; level with a knife. Add 2½ cups flour to yeast mixture, stirring until a soft dough forms. Stir in cranberries and walnuts. Turn dough out onto a lightly floured surface. Knead dough until smooth and elastic (about 5 minutes), adding enough of remaining flour, 1 tablespoon at a time, to prevent dough from sticking to hands.
3. Place dough in a large bowl coated with cooking spray, turning to coat top. Cover and let rise in a warm place (85°), free from drafts, 1 hour or until doubled in size. (Gently press two fingers into dough. If indentation remains, dough has risen enough.)
4. Punch dough down; turn out onto a lightly floured surface. Roll into a 10 x 6–inch rectangle. Starting with a short edge, roll up dough tightly, jelly-roll fashion, pressing firmly to eliminate air pockets; pinch seam and ends to seal. Place roll, seam side down, in a 9 x 5–inch loaf pan coated with cooking spray. Cover and let rise 30 minutes or until doubled in size.
5. Preheat oven to 375°.
6. Bake at 375° for 30 minutes or until top is golden and loaf sounds hollow when tapped. Remove from pan; cool completely on a wire rack. **Yield:** 16 servings (serving size: 1 slice).

Per serving: CALORIES 143; FAT 3.3g (sat 1.2g, mono 0.7g, poly 1.2g); PROTEIN 3.5g; CARB 24.5g; FIBER 1g; CHOL 5mg; IRON 1.2mg; SODIUM 91mg; CALC 24mg

Grocery List

- ☐ 1 (3-packet) strip dry yeast
- ☐ 1 carton 2% reduced-fat milk
- ☐ 1 (5-ounce) bag dried cranberries
- ☐ 1 (2-ounce) bag chopped walnuts
- ☐ Check staples: sugar, salt, butter, flour, cooking spray

Chocolate-Filled Brioche

prep: 36 minutes • **cook:** 15 minutes • **other:** 2 hours and 25 minutes

PointsPlus value per serving: 4

Brioche is a classic French yeast bread made rich with butter and eggs. We've used less butter and fewer eggs than a traditional brioche without sacrificing the rich tenderness.

3   tablespoons sugar, divided
1   package dry yeast (about 2¼ teaspoons)
½   cup warm fat-free milk (100° to 110°)
12.4   ounces all-purpose flour, divided (about 2¾ cups)
1   teaspoon vanilla extract
2   large eggs, divided
1   large egg yolk
1   teaspoon salt
⅓   cup butter, cut into small pieces
Cooking spray
⅓   cup dark chocolate chips

1. Dissolve ¼ teaspoon sugar and yeast in milk. Let stand 5 minutes.

2. Weigh or lightly spoon flour into dry measuring cups; level with a knife. Combine 2½ cups flour and 2 tablespoons plus 2¾ teaspoons sugar in a large bowl; make a well in center of mixture. Add vanilla to milk mixture. Pour milk mixture into well in dry ingredients. Beat with a mixer at medium speed just until combined. Add 1 egg, egg yolk, and salt; beat just until combined. Gradually beat in butter. Turn dough out onto a lightly floured work surface. Knead until smooth and elastic (about 8 minutes), adding enough of remaining flour, 1 tablespoon at a time, to prevent dough from sticking to hands.

3. Place dough in a large bowl coated with cooking spray, turning to coat top. Cover and let rise in a warm place (85°), free from drafts, 1½ hours or until doubled in size. (Gently press two fingers into dough. If indentation remains, dough has risen enough.) Punch dough down; cover and let rest 5 minutes.

4. Divide dough into 16 equal portions; shape portions into balls. Make an indentation in each ball, and tuck about 10 chocolate chips in each indentation. Pull dough over chips, and pinch to enclose chocolate in center of each ball. Place rolls, seam sides down, in muffin cups coated with cooking spray. Cover and let rise 45 minutes or until doubled in size.

5. Preheat oven to 350°.

6. Lightly beat 1 egg; brush tops of rolls with egg. Bake at 350° for 15 minutes or until golden. **Yield:** 16 servings (serving size: 1 roll).

Per serving: CALORIES 165; FAT 6.4g (sat 3.6g, mono 1.4g, poly 0.4g); PROTEIN 3.9g; CARB 22.5g; FIBER 0.7g; CHOL 49mg; IRON 1.2mg; SODIUM 188mg; CALC 19mg

Desserts

pictured on page 124

Dark Chocolate Chunk Cookies

prep: 13 minutes • **cook:** 8 minutes per batch   *PointsPlus* value per serving: 1

You won't believe that each one of these decadent cookies has only 52 calories and a *PointsPlus* value of 1.

 7.5 ounces all-purpose flour (about 1⅔ cups)
 ¾   teaspoon baking soda
 ½   teaspoon salt
 ⅓   cup butter, softened
 1   cup packed brown sugar
 2   teaspoons vanilla extract
 1   large egg
 ¼   cup chopped walnuts, toasted
 4   ounces dark chocolate, coarsely chopped (about ¾ cup)
 Cooking spray

1. Preheat oven to 350°.

2. Weigh or lightly spoon flour into dry measuring cups; level with a knife. Combine flour, baking soda, and salt.

3. Beat butter with a mixer at medium speed until fluffy. Add brown sugar, beating until blended. Add vanilla and egg, beating just until blended.

4. Gradually add flour mixture to butter mixture, stirring just until combined; fold in walnuts and chocolate. Drop by rounded teaspoonfuls 2 inches apart onto baking sheets coated with cooking spray.

5. Bake at 350° for 8 to 10 minutes or until lightly browned. Remove from pans, and cool completely on wire racks. **Yield:** 58 cookies (serving size: 1 cookie).

Per serving: CALORIES 52; FAT 2.1g (sat 1.1g, mono 0.4g, poly 0.3g); PROTEIN 0.7g; CARB 7.7g; FIBER 0.3g; CHOL 7mg; IRON 0.3mg; SODIUM 47mg; CALC 5mg

pictured on page 125

Blueberry-Walnut Oatmeal Cookies

prep: 25 minutes • **cook:** 10 minutes per batch   *PointsPlus* value per serving: 3

Crunchy and sweet, these fruited, fiber-filled cookies are perfect for a snack or even for breakfast on the go.

Grocery List

- ☐ 1 (8-ounce) block ⅓-less-fat cream cheese
- ☐ 1 (18-ounce) canister old-fashioned rolled oats
- ☐ 1 (8-ounce) bag dried blueberries
- ☐ 1 (8-ounce) bag chopped walnuts
- ☐ Check staples: flour, baking soda, salt, unsalted butter, brown sugar, sugar, vanilla, eggs, cooking spray

6.75   ounces all-purpose flour (about 1½ cups)
  1   teaspoon baking soda
  ½   teaspoon salt
  4   ounces ⅓-less-fat cream cheese (about ½ cup), softened
  6   tablespoons unsalted butter, softened
  ¾   cup packed brown sugar
  ½   cup granulated sugar
  2   teaspoons vanilla extract
  1   large egg
2½   cups old-fashioned rolled oats
  1   cup dried blueberries
  1   cup chopped walnuts
    Cooking spray

1. Preheat oven to 350°.

2. Weigh or lightly spoon flour into dry measuring cups; level with a knife. Combine flour, baking soda, and salt.

3. Beat cream cheese and butter with a mixer at medium speed until fluffy. Add sugars, beating until blended. Add vanilla and egg, beating just until blended. Gradually add flour mixture to butter mixture, stirring just until combined. Fold in oats, blueberries, and walnuts. Drop by tablespoonfuls 2 inches apart onto baking sheets coated with cooking spray.

4. Bake at 350° for 10 minutes or until lightly browned. Remove from pans, and cool completely on wire racks. **Yield:** 45 cookies (serving size: 1 cookie).

Per serving: CALORIES 105; FAT 4.2g (sat 1.5g, mono 1g, poly 1.2g); PROTEIN 2.2g; CARB 14.7g; FIBER 1.2g; CHOL 11mg; IRON 0.6mg; SODIUM 70mg; CALC 10mg

pictured on page 126

Lemon Drop Tartlets

prep: 11 minutes • **cook:** 17 minutes

PointsPlus value per serving: 2

Lemon curd contains a higher proportion of lemon juice and rind than lemon filling, so it has a more intense lemon flavor. Its thick, smooth consistency provides a nice balance to the crisp phyllo shells.

1   (2.1-ounce) package mini phyllo shells
⅓   cup lemon curd
2   tablespoons white chocolate chips
1   large egg white
Dash of cream of tartar
2   tablespoons sugar
3   lemon-flavored drop candies

1. Preheat oven to 350°.

2. Place phyllo shells on a baking sheet. Bake at 350° for 3 minutes or until lightly browned and thoroughly heated.

3. Reduce oven temperature to 325°.

4. Combine lemon curd and white chocolate chips in a small microwave-safe bowl. Microwave at HIGH 30 to 40 seconds (chips will not look melted). Stir until morsels melt. Spoon lemon mixture into phyllo shells.

5. Place egg white and cream of tartar in a small bowl; beat with a mixer at high speed until foamy. Gradually add sugar, 1 tablespoon at a time, beating until stiff peaks form. Spoon meringue over lemon mixture, spreading to edges. Bake at 325° for 13 minutes or until meringue is lightly browned.

6. While tartlets bake, place candies in a zip-top plastic bag; seal bag. Crush candies with a meat mallet or small heavy skillet. Remove tartlets from oven, and immediately sprinkle with crushed candies. Cool completely on wire racks.

Yield: 15 servings (serving size: 1 tartlet).

Per serving: CALORIES 59; FAT 1.8g (sat 0.5g, mono 0.7g, poly 0.2g); PROTEIN 0.3g; CARB 10.8g; FIBER 0.7g; CHOL 6mg; IRON 0.2mg; SODIUM 23mg; CALC 3mg

pictured on page 127

Turtle Brownies

prep: 9 minutes • **cook:** 23 minutes   *PointsPlus* value per serving: 4

Indulge your sweet tooth by biting into ooey-gooey caramel pockets in this fudgy treat. Toast the pecans on a baking sheet in an oven preheated to 350° for six minutes.

  1   cup sugar
  ½   cup unsweetened cocoa
  3   tablespoons butter, melted
  2   large egg whites
  1   large egg
  3   ounces all-purpose flour (about ⅔ cup)
  ½   teaspoon baking powder
  ⅛   teaspoon salt
  ¾   cup miniature chocolate-covered chewy caramels
  ⅓   cup chopped pecans, toasted
  Cooking spray

1. Preheat oven to 350°.

2. Combine first 3 ingredients in a large bowl. Add egg whites and egg, stirring until blended.

3. Weigh or lightly spoon flour into dry measuring cups; level with a knife. Combine flour, baking powder, and salt; add to sugar mixture, stirring just until blended. Stir in caramels and pecans. Spread brownie batter into a foil-lined 8-inch square metal baking pan coated with cooking spray.

4. Bake at 350° for 23 to 24 minutes (wooden pick will not test clean). Cool completely in pan on a wire rack. **Yield:** 16 servings (serving size: 1 brownie).

Per serving: CALORIES 134; FAT 5.3g (sat 2.1g, mono 1.7g, poly 0.6g); PROTEIN 2.3g; CARB 20.7g; FIBER 0.8g; CHOL 18mg; IRON 0.8mg; SODIUM 72mg; CALC 12mg

Vanilla and Peach Shortcakes

prep: 10 minutes • **cook:** 9 minutes   *PointsPlus* value per serving: 6

1   pound fresh or frozen peach slices, thawed
¼   cup sugar, divided
1½   teaspoons vanilla extract, divided
1   cup low-fat baking mix
½   teaspoon ground cinnamon
⅓   cup low-fat buttermilk
Cooking spray
1   cup frozen fat-free whipped topping, thawed

1. Preheat oven to 450°.

2. Combine peaches, 2 tablespoons sugar, and 1 teaspoon vanilla in a medium bowl, stirring well. Set aside.

3. Combine baking mix, 2 tablespoons sugar, and cinnamon in a small bowl, stirring well. Add buttermilk and ½ teaspoon vanilla; stir just until blended.

4. Spoon batter onto a baking sheet coated with cooking spray, creating 4 equal mounds. Bake at 450° for 9 minutes or until lightly golden.

5. Carefully cut each shortcake in half crosswise. Spoon ¼ cup peach mixture and ¼ cup whipped topping over bottom half of each shortcake. Replace top halves of shortcakes, and top each serving with ¼ cup peach mixture.

Yield: 4 servings (serving size: 1 shortcake).

Per serving: CALORIES 222; FAT 2.2g (sat 0g, mono 1.2g, poly 0.5g); PROTEIN 4.1g; CARB 47.4g; FIBER 2.2g; CHOL 0mg; IRON 1.5mg; SODIUM 346mg; CALC 149mg

Chocolate Cookie Pudding

prep: 12 minutes • **other:** 10 minutes   *PointsPlus* value per serving: 4

- 2 cups fat-free half-and-half
- 1 (2.1-ounce) package sugar-free chocolate instant pudding mix
- 4 ounces tub-style light cream cheese (about ½ cup), softened
- 1 (8-ounce) container frozen fat-free whipped topping, thawed
- 10 reduced-fat cream-filled chocolate sandwich cookies, coarsely crushed
- ⅓ cup chopped toasted pecans

1. Combine half-and-half and pudding mix in a bowl; stir with a whisk 2 minutes. Cover; chill 10 minutes.
2. While pudding chills, combine cream cheese and whipped topping.
3. Place half of crushed cookies in bottom of a small trifle bowl or other bowl. Spread half of cream cheese mixture over cookies; sprinkle with half of pecans. Spread pudding over top. Spread remaining cream cheese mixture over pudding; sprinkle with remaining cookies and pecans. Cover and chill until ready to serve. **Yield:** 12 servings (serving size: ½ cup).

Per serving: CALORIES 160; FAT 5.6g (sat 1.7g, mono 2.5g, poly 1g); PROTEIN 3.5g; CARB 21.9g; FIBER 1g; CHOL 7mg; IRON 1.2mg; SODIUM 263mg; CALC 66mg

Grocery List

- ☐ 1 (16-ounce) carton fat-free half-and-half
- ☐ 1 (2.1-ounce) package sugar-free chocolate instant pudding mix
- ☐ 1 (8-ounce) tub light cream cheese
- ☐ 1 (8-ounce) container frozen fat-free whipped topping
- ☐ 1 (16.6-ounce) package reduced-fat chocolate sandwich cookies
- ☐ 1 (3-ounce) bag chopped pecans

Banana Pudding

prep: 15 minutes • **other:** 2 hours   *PointsPlus* value per serving: 7

- 2 cups fat-free milk
- 1 (1-ounce) package sugar-free vanilla instant pudding mix
- 4 ounces block-style ⅓-less-fat cream cheese (about ½ cup), softened
- 1 (14-ounce) can fat-free sweetened condensed milk
- 1 (16-ounce) container frozen reduced-calorie whipped topping, thawed and divided
- 56 reduced-fat vanilla wafers
- 4 cups sliced ripe banana (about 4 bananas)

1. Combine fat-free milk and pudding mix in a medium bowl; stir with a whisk 2 minutes. In another bowl, combine cream cheese and sweetened condensed milk, stirring with a whisk until smooth. Fold in 1 cup whipped topping. Fold cream cheese mixture into pudding mixture until blended.
2. Arrange half of vanilla wafers in bottom of a 13 x 9–inch glass or ceramic baking dish. Arrange half of banana slices over wafers. Spread half of pudding mixture over banana. Repeat procedure with remaining wafers, banana, and pudding mixture. Top with remaining whipped topping. Cover and refrigerate 2 hours or until thoroughly chilled. **Yield:** 16 servings (serving size: about ¾ cup).

Per serving: CALORIES 254; FAT 6.3g (sat 4.3g, mono 0.3g, poly 0.1g); PROTEIN 5.4g; CARB 44.6g; FIBER 1g; CHOL 9mg; IRON 0.5mg; SODIUM 233mg; CALC 129mg

Grocery List

- ☐ 1 (1-ounce) package sugar-free vanilla instant pudding mix
- ☐ 1 (8-ounce) block ⅓-less-fat cream cheese
- ☐ 1 (14-ounce) can fat-free sweetened condensed milk
- ☐ 1 (16-ounce) container frozen reduced-calorie whipped topping
- ☐ 1 (11-ounce) box reduced-fat vanilla wafers
- ☐ 4 ripe bananas
- ☐ Check staple: fat-free milk

Coffee Crème Brûlée

prep: 12 minutes • **cook:** 62 minutes • **other:** 8 hours and 20 minutes

PointsPlus value per serving: 5

The secret to a crisp caramelized crust on top is to make sure the custard's surface is dry. Use paper towels to lightly dab away excess moisture before sprinkling the custards with sugar.

½ cup nonfat dry milk
½ cup fat-free half-and-half
1 tablespoon instant coffee granules
1 (12-ounce) can evaporated fat-free milk
3 tablespoons plus 5 teaspoons sugar, divided
2 (3-inch) cinnamon sticks
⅛ teaspoon salt
4 large egg yolks

1. Combine first 4 ingredients and 2 tablespoons sugar in a medium saucepan; add cinnamon sticks. Cook over medium heat 7 minutes or until hot, stirring occasionally. Remove from heat. Cover and let stand 20 minutes. Discard cinnamon sticks.
2. Preheat oven to 300°.
3. Combine 1 tablespoon sugar, salt, and egg yolks in a medium bowl, stirring with a whisk. Gradually add milk mixture, stirring with whisk. Pour custard mixture into 5 (4-ounce) ramekins or custard cups. Place ramekins in a 13 x 9–inch metal baking pan; add hot water to pan to a depth of 1 inch.
4. Bake at 300° for 50 minutes or until center barely moves when ramekin is touched. Cool custards in water in pan on a wire rack. Remove ramekins from pan; cover and chill at least 8 hours or overnight.
5. Carefully pat the surface of each custard cup dry with paper towels. Sprinkle 1 teaspoon sugar over each custard. Holding a kitchen blowtorch about 2 inches from top of 1 custard, heat sugar, moving torch back and forth, until sugar is completely melted and caramelized (about 1 minute). Repeat procedure with remaining custard cups. Serve immediately or within 1 hour. **Yield:** 5 servings (serving size: 1 crème brûlée).

Per serving: CALORIES 181; FAT 4g (sat 1.6g, mono 1.6g, poly 0.6g); PROTEIN 10.4g; CARB 25.9g; FIBER 0g; CHOL 169mg; IRON 0.6mg; SODIUM 215mg; CALC 329mg

Pumpkin Custards with Brittle Topping

prep: 7 minutes • **cook:** 45 minutes • **other:** 8 hours

PointsPlus value per serving: 7

Crunchy peanut brittle and a smooth and creamy pumpkin mixture create a perfect marriage of textures in these heavenly custards.

1   teaspoon pumpkin pie spice
2   teaspoons vanilla extract
⅛   teaspoon salt
4   large eggs
1   (15-ounce) can pumpkin
1   (14-ounce) can fat-free sweetened condensed milk
Cooking spray
¼   cup chopped peanut brittle

1. Preheat oven to 325°.
2. Place first 6 ingredients in a blender; process just until smooth. Pour custard mixture into 6 (6-ounce) ramekins or custard cups coated with cooking spray. Place ramekins in a 13 x 9–inch metal baking pan; add hot water to pan to a depth of 1 inch.
3. Bake at 325° for 45 minutes or until center barely moves when ramekin is touched. Remove ramekins from pan; cool completely on a wire rack. Cover and chill at least 8 hours. Sprinkle each custard with 2 teaspoons peanut brittle before serving. **Yield:** 6 servings (serving size: 1 custard).

Per serving: CALORIES 288; FAT 4.2g (sat 1.3g, mono 1.3g, poly 0.5g); PROTEIN 10.5g; CARB 51g; FIBER 2.2g; CHOL 149mg; IRON 1.7mg; SODIUM 210mg; CALC 208mg

---

Grocery List

☐ 1 (1-ounce) bottle pumpkin pie spice
☐ 1 (15-ounce) can pumpkin
☐ 1 (14-ounce) can fat-free sweetened condensed milk
☐ 1 small bag or box peanut brittle
☐ Check staples: vanilla, salt, eggs, cooking spray

White Chocolate Panna Cotta

prep: 4 minutes • **cook:** 3 minutes • **other:** 8 hours and 1 minute

PointsPlus value per serving: 7

Panna cotta is an Italian dessert made of heavy cream and served with either berries, caramel topping, or chocolate sauce. We substituted fat-free half-and-half and fat-free sweetened condensed milk for the heavy cream and added a little white chocolate for flavor.

  1 envelope unflavored gelatin
  2 cups fat-free half-and-half, divided
  3 ounces white chocolate, chopped
  1 cup fat-free sweetened condensed milk
  ½ teaspoon vanilla extract
  Fresh raspberries (optional)

1. Sprinkle gelatin over 1 cup half-and-half in a small saucepan; let stand 1 to 2 minutes. Cook, stirring constantly, over medium heat 3 minutes or until gelatin dissolves; remove from heat. Add chocolate, stirring until it melts.
2. Gradually stir in 1 cup half-and-half, condensed milk, and vanilla. Pour ½ cup custard into each of 6 stemmed glasses or 6-ounce custard cups. Cover and chill 8 hours. Serve with berries, if desired. **Yield:** 6 servings (serving size: 1 panna cotta).

Per serving: CALORIES 281; FAT 4.6g (sat 2.8g, mono 1.2g, poly 0.1g); PROTEIN 5.8g; CARB 48.4g; FIBER 0g; CHOL 9mg; IRON 0.1mg; SODIUM 148mg; CALC 216mg

Frozen Berries-and-Cream Pops

prep: 10 minutes • **other:** 2 hours   *PointsPlus* value per serving: 1

  2 cups sliced strawberries
  ½ cup evaporated fat-free milk
  3 tablespoons corn syrup
  3 tablespoons frozen cranberry juice concentrate, thawed
  1 tablespoon vanilla extract

1. Combine all ingredients in a blender; process until smooth. Pour mixture into 8 (3-ounce) wax-coated paper cups. Place a wooden craft stick in center of each cup. Place prepared cups on a baking sheet, and freeze at least 2 hours or until firm. To release pops from cups, dip cups into hot water almost to rims of cups. **Yield:** 8 servings (serving size: 1 pop).

Per serving: CALORIES 55; FAT 0.2g (sat 0g, mono 0g, poly 0.1g); PROTEIN 1.5g; CARB 11.8g; FIBER 0.8g; CHOL 1mg; IRON 0.2mg; SODIUM 24mg; CALC 54mg

Chocolate Cream Pie

prep: 9 minutes • **cook:** 8 minutes • **other:** 3 hours and 5 minutes

PointsPlus value per serving: 6

Adding melted dark chocolate chips to a store-bought pudding mix is the secret to this decadent shortcut cream pie.

2   cups fat-free milk
2   (1.3-ounce) packages sugar-free chocolate cook-and-serve pudding mix
¼   cup dark chocolate chips
1   (6-ounce) reduced-fat graham cracker crust
1   (8-ounce) container frozen fat-free whipped topping, thawed

1. Combine milk and pudding mixes in a medium saucepan, stirring well with a whisk. Cook over medium heat 8 minutes or until mixture comes to a boil, stirring constantly. Remove from heat, and add chocolate chips, stirring until chocolate melts. Place pan in an ice-water bath 5 minutes or until cool, stirring often.
2. Pour filling into crust. Cover surface of filling with plastic wrap, and chill at least 3 hours. Spread whipped topping over pie before serving. **Yield:** 8 servings (serving size: 1 slice).

Per serving: CALORIES 214; FAT 5.8g (sat 1.8g, mono 0.5g, poly 0.1g); PROTEIN 3.8g; CARB 34.5g; FIBER 0.4g; CHOL 1mg; IRON 0.3mg; SODIUM 253mg; CALC 77mg

Grocery List

- [ ] 2 (1.3-ounce) packages sugar-free chocolate cook-and-serve pudding mix
- [ ] 1 (10-ounce) bag dark chocolate chips
- [ ] 1 (6-ounce) reduced-fat graham cracker crust
- [ ] 1 (8-ounce) container frozen fat-free whipped topping
- [ ] Check staple: fat-free milk

Key Lime Pie Ice Cream

prep: 13 minutes • **other:** 2 hours and 25 minutes   *PointsPlus* value per serving: 6

1   cup fat-free half-and-half
1   cup half-and-half
½   cup Key lime juice
1   (14-ounce) can low-fat sweetened condensed milk
24   low-fat graham crackers (6 full cookie sheets), coarsely crushed
1   (7-ounce) can refrigerated fat-free dairy whipped topping

1. Combine first 4 ingredients, stirring with a whisk.
2. Pour mixture into the freezer can of a 2-quart ice-cream freezer, and freeze according to manufacturer's instructions.
3. Spoon ice cream alternately with crushed graham crackers and whipped topping into a freezer-safe container; cover and freeze 2 hours or until firm. **Yield:** 10 servings (serving size: ½ cup).

Per serving: CALORIES 230; FAT 5g (sat 2.9g, mono 0.8g, poly 0g); PROTEIN 4.9g; CARB 37.3g; FIBER 0.3g; CHOL 15mg; IRON 0.3mg; SODIUM 137mg; CALC 191mg

Grocery List

- [ ] 1 (16-ounce) carton fat-free half-and-half
- [ ] 1 (16-ounce) carton half-and-half
- [ ] 1 (8-ounce) bottle Key lime juice
- [ ] 1 (14-ounce) can low-fat sweetened condensed milk
- [ ] 1 (14.4-ounce) box low-fat graham crackers
- [ ] 1 (7-ounce) can refrigerated fat-free dairy whipped topping

pictured on page 128

Caramel Apple Galette

prep: 7 minutes • **cook:** 21 minutes   *PointsPlus* value per serving: 4

Grocery List

- ☐ 1 box light stick butter
- ☐ 2 large Granny Smith apples
- ☐ 1 (13.8-ounce) can refrigerated pizza crust dough
- ☐ 1 (16-ounce) bag turbinado sugar
- ☐ 1 (12.25-ounce) jar sugar-free caramel topping
- ☐ Check staple: cooking spray

1   tablespoon light stick butter
3   cups thinly sliced peeled Granny Smith apple (about 2 large)
Cooking spray
1   (13.8-ounce) can refrigerated pizza crust dough
3   tablespoons turbinado sugar
½   cup sugar-free caramel topping

1. Preheat oven to 425°.

2. Melt butter in a large nonstick skillet over medium-high heat. Add apple slices; sauté 3 to 4 minutes or until tender and golden.

3. Line a baking sheet with parchment paper; spray paper with cooking spray. Unroll dough onto sprayed parchment; pat dough into a 13-inch circle. Spoon apple slices onto dough, leaving a 2-inch border. Fold dough over filling, forming a 2-inch border of dough that partially covers filling. Press dough gently against filling. Sprinkle filling with turbinado sugar.

4. Bake at 425° for 17 minutes or until crust is golden and apples are tender. Let galette cool slightly on pan before cutting into 12 wedges. Drizzle each serving with caramel topping just before serving. **Yield:** 12 servings (serving size: 1 wedge and 2 teaspoons topping).

Per serving: CALORIES 135; FAT 1.5g (sat 0.5g, mono 0.3g, poly 0.5g); PROTEIN 2.6g; CARB 29.4g; FIBER 0.9g; CHOL 1mg; IRON 0.9mg; SODIUM 265mg; CALC 1mg

Apple Crepes with Caramel Topping

prep: 2 minutes • **cook:** 5 minutes   *PointsPlus* value per serving: 8

Grocery List

- ☐ 1 (12-ounce) package frozen apples
- ☐ 1 (1-ounce) bottle apple pie spice
- ☐ 1 package ready-to-use crepes
- ☐ 1 pint vanilla low-fat ice cream
- ☐ 1 (12.25-ounce) jar fat-free caramel topping
- ☐ Check staple: brown sugar

1   (12-ounce) package frozen apples
2   teaspoons brown sugar
¼   teaspoon apple pie spice
3   ready-to-use crepes
1   cup vanilla low-fat ice cream
3   tablespoons fat-free caramel topping

1. Prepare apples according to package directions.

2. Sprinkle brown sugar and apple pie spice over apples; stir well. Spoon ⅓ cup apple mixture onto center of each crepe. Roll up crepes. Place crepes on a microwave-safe plate.

3. Microwave at HIGH 10 seconds or until heated.

4. Top each crepe with ⅓ cup ice cream and 1 tablespoon caramel topping. Serve immediately. **Yield:** 3 servings (serving size: 1 crepe).

Per serving: CALORIES 286; FAT 3.5g (sat 1g, mono 0.3g, poly 0.1g); PROTEIN 2.5g; CARB 62.7g; FIBER 3.9g; CHOL 9mg; IRON 0.3mg; SODIUM 148mg; CALC 70mg

Lemon-Raspberry Cupcakes

prep: 19 minutes • **cook:** 17 minutes

PointsPlus value per serving: 2

Tangy lemon juice and sweet raspberry preserves make a refreshing filling for these cupcakes.

- 1 (16-ounce) package angel food cake mix
- 1 teaspoon vanilla extract
- ¾ cup low-sugar seedless raspberry preserves, divided
- 1½ teaspoons grated fresh lemon rind
- 3½ tablespoons fresh lemon juice, divided
- 2 cups powdered sugar

1. Preheat oven to 375°.

2. Prepare cake mix according to package directions. Stir in vanilla.

3. Place 33 foil muffin cup liners on a large baking sheet, or place in muffin cups. Divide batter among muffin cup liners, filling about two-thirds full.

4. Bake at 375° for 17 to 18 minutes or until cupcakes are golden brown and cracks in cakes appear dry.

5. Set aside 1 tablespoon raspberry preserves. Combine ½ cup plus 3 tablespoons raspberry preserves, lemon rind, and 1 tablespoon lemon juice in a bowl, stirring until smooth; set aside.

6. Combine powdered sugar and 2½ tablespoons lemon juice, stirring with a whisk until smooth. Add reserved 1 tablespoon raspberry preserves to lemon juice glaze; swirl together with a knife.

7. Cut a deep slit in top center of each cake to form a pocket. Carefully spoon 1 heaping teaspoonful raspberry filling into each warm cake. Spoon 1 tablespoon lemon juice glaze over each cupcake. **Yield:** 33 servings (serving size: 1 cupcake).

Per serving: CALORIES 89; FAT 0.1g; PROTEIN 1.2g; CARB 21.3g; FIBER 0.1g; CHOL 0mg; IRON 0.1mg; SODIUM 101mg; CALC 17mg

Grocery List

- ☐ 1 (16-ounce) package angel food cake mix
- ☐ 1 (12-ounce) jar low-sugar seedless raspberry preserves
- ☐ 1 large lemon
- ☐ 1 (1-pound) box powdered sugar
- ☐ Check staple: vanilla

Grocery List

- ☐ 1 (16-ounce) package angel food cake mix
- ☐ 1 (20-ounce) can light apple pie filling
- ☐ 1 (16-ounce) carton fat-free half-and-half
- ☐ 1 (18-ounce) box low-fat granola
- ☐ Check staples: vanilla, brown sugar, butter

French Apple Cupcakes

prep: 17 minutes • **cook:** 17 minutes   *PointsPlus* value per serving: 4

With a soothing combination of gooey apple pie filling, a warm caramel glaze, and crunchy granola, each of these cupcakes is like a cobbler in a cup.

  1 (16-ounce) package angel food cake mix
  1 teaspoon vanilla extract
  2 cups light apple pie filling
     Caramel Glaze
1⅓ cups low-fat granola

1. Preheat oven to 375°.

2. Prepare cake mix according to package directions. Stir in vanilla.

3. Place 33 foil muffin cup liners on a large baking sheet, or place in muffin cups. Divide batter among liners, filling about two-thirds full.

4. Bake at 375° for 17 to 18 minutes or until cupcakes are golden brown and cracks in cakes appear dry.

5. Chop apple pie filling in a food processor. Set aside.

6. Cut a deep slit in top center of each cake to form a pocket. Carefully spoon 1 tablespoon chopped apple pie filling into each warm cake.

7. Spoon about 2½ teaspoons Caramel Glaze over each cake. Sprinkle about 2 teaspoons granola over each cupcake. **Yield:** 33 servings (serving size: 1 cupcake).

Per serving: CALORIES 154; FAT 0.7g (sat 0.3g, mono 0.1g, poly 0g); PROTEIN 1.7g; CARB 36.1g; FIBER 0.5g; CHOL 1mg; IRON 0.7mg; SODIUM 129mg; CALC 39mg

Caramel Glaze

prep: 3 minutes • **cook:** 7 minutes • **other:** 5 minutes

PointsPlus value per serving: 3

  3 cups packed brown sugar
  ¾ cup fat-free half-and-half
  1 tablespoon butter
  1 tablespoon vanilla extract

1. Combine sugar and half-and-half in a saucepan, stirring with a whisk. Bring to a boil over medium heat; cook 2 minutes or until sugar dissolves. Stir in butter and vanilla. Cool slightly. **Yield:** about 1¾ cups (serving size: 2½ teaspoons).

Per serving: CALORIES 83; FAT 0.4g (sat 0.2g, mono 0g, poly 0g); PROTEIN 0.2g; CARB 20.1g; FIBER 0g; CHOL 1mg; IRON 0.4mg; SODIUM 18mg; CALC 22mg

Mint Chocolate Cupcakes

prep: 15 minutes • **cook:** 26 minutes • **other:** 40 minutes

PointsPlus **value per serving: 3**

Cooking spray
1   (18.25-ounce) package devil's food cake mix
1   (12-ounce) can cola
⅔   cup crème de menthe baking chips, divided
1   tablespoon evaporated low-fat milk
1   (8-ounce) container frozen fat-free whipped topping, thawed

1. Preheat oven to 350°.
2. Place 24 paper muffin cup liners in muffin cups. Coat liners with cooking spray. Place cake mix and cola in a large bowl. Beat with a mixer at low speed just until moist. Beat 2 minutes at medium speed or until batter is smooth. Stir in ⅓ cup baking chips. Spoon batter into prepared muffin cup liners.
3. Bake at 350° for 25 minutes or until cupcakes spring back when touched lightly in center. Cool in pans on wire racks 5 minutes. Remove from pans. Cool cupcakes on wire racks 35 minutes or until completely cool.
4. Place ⅓ cup baking chips and milk in a large microwave-safe bowl. Microwave at HIGH 30 seconds; stir until smooth. Fold in whipped topping. Spoon over cupcakes. **Yield:** 24 servings (serving size: 1 cupcake).

Per serving: CALORIES 128; FAT 3.1g (sat 1.5g, mono 0.9g, poly 0.7g); PROTEIN 1.2g; CARB 23.6g; FIBER 0.6g; CHOL 0mg; IRON 0.9mg; SODIUM 195mg; CALC 30mg

Grocery List

- ☐ 1 (18.25-ounce) package devil's food cake mix
- ☐ 1 (12-ounce) can cola
- ☐ 1 (8-ounce) package crème de menthe baking chips
- ☐ 1 (5-ounce) can evaporated low-fat milk
- ☐ 1 (8-ounce) container frozen fat-free whipped topping
- ☐ Check staple: cooking spray

Chocolate Sponge Cake Cupcakes

prep: 10 minutes • **cook:** 19 minutes • **other:** 30 minutes

PointsPlus value per serving: 4

Cooking spray
4.5 ounces all-purpose flour (about 1 cup)
3 tablespoons Dutch process cocoa
1 teaspoon baking powder
¼ teaspoon salt
½ cup 1% low-fat milk
2 tablespoons light stick butter
1 cup sugar
2 large eggs
2 teaspoons vanilla extract
1½ cups frozen fat-free whipped topping, thawed

1. Preheat oven to 350°.
2. Place 12 paper muffin cup liners in muffin cups; coat liners with cooking spray. Set aside.
3. Weigh or lightly spoon flour into a dry measuring cup; level with a knife. Sift together flour and next 3 ingredients.
4. Combine milk and butter in a 1-cup glass measure, and microwave at HIGH 1 to 1½ minutes or until butter melts.
5. Beat sugar and eggs with a mixer at high speed 5 minutes. Add flour mixture, milk mixture, and vanilla. Beat at medium speed 30 seconds or until smooth. Spoon batter into prepared muffin cups.
6. Bake at 350° for 18 minutes or until cupcakes spring back when touched lightly in center. Cool cupcakes in pan on a wire rack 10 minutes; remove from pan, and cool completely. Spoon 2 tablespoons whipped topping onto each cupcake just before serving. **Yield:** 12 cupcakes (serving size: 1 cupcake).

Per serving: CALORIES 150; FAT 3.3g (sat 0.9g, mono 0.4g, poly 0.2g); PROTEIN 2.7g; CARB 28.3g; FIBER 0.5g; CHOL 38mg; IRON 1.1mg; SODIUM 127mg; CALC 41mg

Upside-Down Pineapple Spice Cake

prep: 11 minutes • **cook:** 50 minutes • **other:** 25 minutes

PointsPlus value per serving: 5

Adding mashed banana to the cake mix makes this dessert very moist. To mash the banana easily, place it in a zip-top plastic bag and squeeze until the banana is well mashed; then add it to the other ingredients in the bowl as directed.

Grocery List

- [ ] 1 (16-ounce) carton egg substitute
- [ ] 1 medium-sized ripe banana
- [ ] 1 (18.25-ounce) package spice cake mix
- [ ] 1 (20-ounce) can pineapple slices in juice
- [ ] 1 box light stick butter
- [ ] Check staples: canola oil, cooking spray, brown sugar, cornstarch, vanilla

  1⅓ cups water
  ¾   cup egg substitute
  ¼   cup mashed ripe banana (about ½ medium)
  2   tablespoons canola oil
  1   (18.25-ounce) package spice cake mix
  1   (20-ounce) can pineapple slices in juice, undrained
      Cooking spray
  2   tablespoons brown sugar
  1¼ teaspoons cornstarch
  1   tablespoon light stick butter
  1   teaspoon vanilla extract

1. Preheat oven to 325°.

2. Combine first 5 ingredients in a large bowl; beat with a mixer at medium speed until well blended. Set aside.

3. Drain pineapple slices into a bowl, reserving ¾ cup juice. Press pineapple slices between paper towels until barely moist; cut in half. Arrange prepared pineapple slices in a single layer in a 9½-inch nonstick springform pan coated with cooking spray.

4. Pour batter over pineapple slices. Bake at 325° for 48 minutes or until a wooden pick inserted in center comes out almost clean. Cool in pan 10 minutes on a wire rack. Invert cake onto wire rack, and cool completely.

5. While cake cools, combine reserved pineapple juice, sugar, and cornstarch in a medium saucepan, stirring constantly with a whisk until cornstarch dissolves. Place juice mixture over medium-high heat; bring to a boil. Boil 1 minute, stirring constantly. Remove from heat, and stir in butter and vanilla. Cool 15 minutes. Transfer cooled cake to a serving plate. Pour cooled sauce over cake. **Yield:** 16 servings (serving size: 1 slice).

Per serving: CALORIES 177; FAT 3.5g (sat 1.2g, mono 1.3g, poly 0.5g); PROTEIN 2.7g; CARB 34.2g; FIBER 0.4g; CHOL 1mg; IRON 0.9mg; SODIUM 242mg; CALC 66mg

Triple-Layer Mocha Toffee Cake

prep: 24 minutes • **cook:** 20 minutes • **other:** 60 minutes

PointsPlus **value per serving: 7**

Cooking spray
⅓ cup Dutch process cocoa
1½ teaspoons baking powder
¼ teaspoon salt
6 ounces cake flour (about 1½ cups)
⅔ cup 1% low-fat milk
3 tablespoons light stick butter
1½ cups plus 2 tablespoons sugar, divided
3 large eggs
2 teaspoons vanilla extract
2 teaspoons instant espresso granules
3 tablespoons coffee-flavored liqueur
3 tablespoons water
1 (8-ounce) container frozen chocolate whipped topping, thawed
3 (1.4-ounce) chocolate-covered toffee bars, finely chopped

1. Preheat oven to 350°.

2. Line 3 (8-inch) cake pans with parchment paper; coat with cooking spray. Set pans aside.

3. Sift together cocoa and next 3 ingredients.

4. Combine milk and butter in a 2-cup glass measure. Microwave at HIGH 1 to 1½ minutes or until mixture is very hot.

5. Beat 1½ cups sugar and eggs with a mixer at high speed 5 minutes or until egg mixture is pale yellow and thick. Add flour mixture, milk mixture, and vanilla. Beat 30 seconds or until well combined (batter will be thin). Quickly pour batter into prepared cake pans.

6. Bake at 350° for 18 to 20 minutes or until cakes start to pull away from sides of pans and spring back when touched lightly in center. Cool in pans on wire racks 10 minutes. Remove from pans, and cool completely.

7. Combine espresso granules, coffee liqueur, 2 tablespoons sugar, and 3 table-spoons water in a 1-cup glass measure. Microwave at HIGH 1 minute or until sugar dissolves. Brush coffee mixture over cake layers, allowing syrup to soak into cake. Place 1 cake layer on a cake plate. Spread with about 1 cup whipped topping; sprinkle with ¼ cup chopped toffee bars. Repeat procedure twice with remaining ingredients, ending with toffee bars. **Yield:** 16 servings (serving size: 1 slice).

Per serving: CALORIES 246; FAT 8.7g (sat 4.8g, mono 1.1g, poly 0.3g); PROTEIN 3.2g; CARB 40.7g; FIBER 0.7g; CHOL 47mg; IRON 1.8mg; SODIUM 143mg; CALC 57mg

Index

10 Simple Side Dishes

Vegetable	Servings	Preparation	Cooking Instructions
Asparagus	3 to 4 per pound	Snap off tough ends. Remove scales, if desired.	To steam: Cook, covered, on a rack above boiling water 2 to 3 minutes. To boil: Cook, covered, in a small amount of boiling water 2 to 3 minutes or until crisp-tender.
Broccoli	3 to 4 per pound	Remove outer leaves and tough ends of lower stalks. Wash; cut into spears.	To steam: Cook, covered, on a rack above boiling water 5 to 7 minutes or until crisp-tender.
Carrots	4 per pound	Scrape; remove ends, and rinse. Leave tiny carrots whole; slice large carrots.	To steam: Cook, covered, on a rack above boiling water 8 to 10 minutes or until crisp-tender. To boil: Cook, covered, in a small amount of boiling water 8 to 10 minutes or until crisp-tender.
Cauliflower	4 per medium head	Remove outer leaves and stalk. Wash. Break into florets.	To steam: Cook, covered, on a rack above boiling water 5 to 7 minutes or until crisp-tender.
Corn	4 per 4 large ears	Remove husks and silks. Leave corn on the cob, or cut off kernels.	Cook, covered, in boiling water to cover 8 to 10 minutes (on cob) or in a small amount of boiling water 4 to 6 minutes (kernels).
Green beans	4 per pound	Wash; trim ends, and remove strings. Cut into 1½-inch pieces.	To steam: Cook, covered, on a rack above boiling water 5 to 7 minutes. To boil: Cook, covered, in a small amount of boiling water 5 to 7 minutes or until crisp-tender.
Potatoes	3 to 4 per pound	Scrub; peel, if desired. Leave whole, slice, or cut into chunks.	To boil: Cook, covered, in boiling water to cover 30 to 40 minutes (whole) or 15 to 20 minutes (slices or chunks). To bake: Bake at 400° for 1 hour or until done.
Snow peas	4 per pound	Wash; trim ends, and remove tough strings.	To steam: Cook, covered, on a rack above boiling water 2 to 3 minutes. Or sauté in cooking spray or 1 teaspoon oil over medium-high heat 3 to 4 minutes or until crisp-tender.
Squash, summer	3 to 4 per pound	Wash; trim ends, and slice or chop.	To steam: Cook, covered, on a rack above boiling water 6 to 8 minutes. To boil: Cook, covered, in a small amount of boiling water 6 to 8 minutes or until crisp-tender.
Squash, winter *(including acorn, butternut, and buttercup)*	2 per pound	Rinse; cut in half, and remove all seeds. Leave in halves to bake, or peel and cube to boil.	To boil: Cook cubes, covered, in boiling water 20 to 25 minutes. To bake: Place halves, cut sides down, in a shallow baking dish; add ½ inch water. Bake, uncovered, at 375° for 30 minutes. Turn and season, or fill; bake an additional 20 to 30 minutes or until tender.